Earl Wilson, *The New York Times*

PAMELA PAUL is the editor of *The New York Times
Book Review* and the author of *By the Book*; *Parenting, Inc.*; *Pornified*; and *The Starter Marriage and
the Future of Matrimony*. Prior to joining the *Times*,
she was a contributor to *Time* magazine and *The
Economist*, and her work has appeared in *The Atlantic*, *The Washington Post*, *Slate*, and *Vogue*.

Also by Pamela Paul

By the Book:
Writers on Literature and the Literary Life
from The New York Times Book Review

Parenting, Inc.:
How the Billion-Dollar Baby Business
Has Changed the Way We Raise Our Children

Pornified:
How Pornography Is Transforming Our Lives,
Our Relationships, and Our Families

The Starter Marriage and the Future of Matrimony

Additional Praise for *My Life with Bob*

"[Pamela Paul] is reflective, open, and at times achingly funny. *My Life with Bob* is the book that she was put on this earth to write."
—*The Economist*

"Pamela Paul recalls the stories that have given shape to her own narrative, in her appealingly roving memoir . . . which includes . . . undersung marvels that boldly take measure of the world—and challenge us to write our own story."
—*Vogue*

"An engaging and . . . funny memoir . . . A delightfully gushing love letter to books—books as a medium that can connect us, transport us, and transform us."
—*The Washington Post*

"Bob becomes a memory keeper, not so much of the books . . . as of the personal associations they hold for her, such as the place where she read them or the people she was with at the time. Paul approaches books with tenderness, desire, insecurity, and, always, ambition."
—*The New Yorker*

"A rollicking, intimate expedition through a brilliant booklover's heart, mind, and life."
—*The Christian Science Monitor*

"A heartwarming reminiscence of the books that reflected and shaped her state of mind at every stage of life. By the end, you'll be hard-pressed to not start keeping a 'Bob' . . . of your own."
—*Harper's Bazaar*

"A bibliophile's treasure trove of insights."
—*O, The Oprah Magazine*

"Reading Paul, I began to see how much the books you gravitate toward reveal about your truest loves, your most instinctive urges, as well as more thoughtful, curated appetites. . . . [It's] a baring of one's soul that merits respect." —*Financial Times*

"The ultimate book about reading books." —*BuzzFeed*

"Downright delightful." —*San Francisco Chronicle*

"A smart, beautifully written memoir about the relationship we have with books and how the books we read frame our lives. This charmer is a must for every beach bag this summer." —*PopSugar*

"Compelling, authentic, and every dream of every woman who puts reading before eating, the stories offer a perspective on life. . . . Perfection in a book, *My Life with Bob* is a love story for readers and women who love books too much!" —*The Review Broads*

"A witty, heartfelt, deeply optimistic narrative . . . Titles about reading and books abound, but this memoir stands in a class by itself. Bibliophiles will treasure, but the addictive storytelling and high-quality writing will vastly increase its audience." —*Library Journal* (starred review)

"Intelligent, unique, and wise, Paul's book not only remembers a life lived among and influenced by books. It also reveals how the most interesting stories exist less as words printed on pages and more as 'stories that lie between book and reader.' A thoughtfully engaging memoir of a life in books." —*Kirkus Reviews*

"Paul is inspired to question why we read, how we read, what we read, and how reading helps us create our own narratives. Readers will be drawn to this witty and authentic tribute to the extraordinary power of books."

—*Publishers Weekly* (starred review)

"What makes Paul's narrative absorbing and resonant is her determination: we observe her journeying toward the life she always wanted to have, by reading her way through it."

—*The Times Literary Supplement*

"Pamela Paul's *My Life with Bob* is absolutely essential for those of us to whom books are more or less everything. This is a book I was born to read!" —Robert Gottlieb

"A sweet and heady book that casts a serious charm. Our lively and fetching heroine's journey becomes more thrilling by the page, as Pamela Paul perfectly captures the joys of a lifetime devoted to books, as well as the attendant pressure, doubt, and insecurity. Reading this memoir is pure pleasure—funny, brainy, far-reaching—but more than anything, it feels like a call to arms to recommit to our best self: the book person."

—Maria Semple

"In this hilarious, wise, and elegiac account of a life led half in the world and half in books, Pamela Paul writes with courage and exuberance about the bumpy road to maturity. Her voice—tender, moral, madcap, nostalgic, generous—will captivate all but the most stony reader. *My Life with Bob* is full of hope, full of love, a joyful and poignant reflection on the well-written sentence and the well-lived life." —Andrew Solomon

"Any book that helps me remember reading the Betsy-Tacy and Tib series as well as *A Portrait of the Artist as a Young Man*, is a book I like. Pamela Paul's *My Life with Bob* is an absorbing, delightful amalgam—it's a recommended reading list, a personal reflection, and a paean to reading. I'm sorry I never wrote down all the books I read (or even practically any), but I'm so glad Pamela Paul did." —Meg Wolitzer

My Life with Bob

Date	Author	Title
July/August 88	+ Kafka	The Trial.
	+ Vonnegut	Slaughterhouse Five
	* Walter Lord	A Night to Remember
	* Daniel Keyes	Flowers for Algernon
	* King	Salem's Lot (French trans.)
September 88	Hawthorne	Scarlet Letter
	Twain	Huckleberry Finn
	Crane	Red Badge of Courage
	Malamud	The Assistant
	Conrad	Heart of Darkness
	Faulkner	Go Down Moses
	James	Turn of the Screw
	Joyce	"The Dead"
	Joyce	Portrait of the Artist
	Fitzgerald	The Great Gatsby
	* Rice	Interview with the Vampire (inc.)
	* Sugarman	Nobody Here Gets Out Alive
	* Vonnegut	Breakfast of Champions (inc.)
	* Lawrence	Lady Chatterly's Lover (inc.)
	* Bernhardt	Confessions of a Pretty Lady

My Life with Bob

FLAWED HEROINE

KEEPS BOOK OF BOOKS,

PLOT ENSUES

Pamela Paul

PICADOR   HENRY HOLT AND COMPANY   NEW YORK

MY LIFE WITH BOB. Copyright © 2017 by Pamela Paul. All rights reserved. Printed in the United States of America. For information, address Picador, 175 Fifth Avenue, New York, N.Y. 10010.

picadorusa.com • instagram.com/picador
twitter.com/picadorusa • facebook.com/picadorusa

Picador® is a U.S. registered trademark and is used by Macmillan Publishing Group, LLC, under license from Pan Books Limited.

For book club information, please visit facebook.com/picadorbookclub or email marketing@picadorusa.com.

"Love Song," translation copyright © 1982 by Stephen Mitchell; from Selected Poetry of Rainer Maria Rilke by Rainer Maria Rilke, translated by Stephen Mitchell. Used by permission of Random House, an imprint and division of Penguin Random House LLC. All rights reserved.

Designed by Meryl Sussman Levavi

The Library of Congress has cataloged the Henry Holt and Company edition as follows:

Names: Paul, Pamela.
Title: My life with Bob : flawed heroine keeps book of books, plot ensues / Pamela Paul.
Description: First edition. | New York : Henry Holt and Company, 2017.
Identifiers: LCCN 2016046990 | ISBN 9781627796316 (hardcover) | ISBN 9781627796323 (ebook)
Subjects: LCSH: Paul, Pamela—Books and reading. | Books and reading—Psychological aspects. | BISAC: BIOGRAPHY & AUTOBIOGRAPHY / Personal Memoirs. | LITERARY CRITICISM / Books & Reading. | LITERARY COLLECTIONS / Essays.
Classification: LCC PN4874.P363 A3 2017 | DDC 818'.603 [B]—dc23
LC record available at https://lccn.loc.gov/2016046990

Picador Paperback ISBN 978-1-250-18254-8

Our books may be purchased in bulk for promotional, educational, or business use. Please contact your local bookseller or the Macmillan Corporate and Premium Sales Department at 1-800-221-7945, extension 5442, or by email at MacmillanSpecialMarkets@macmillan.com.

First published by Henry Holt and Company, LLC

First Picador Edition: May 2018

10 9 8 7 6 5 4 3 2 1

To my family of readers,
and in memory of my father

Contents

CONTENTS

Introduction

Why Keep Track?

Like anyone else with a marriage and a home and children and family and work, and more work, I always have something to worry about. And if for some inexplicable reason, I don't have anything to fret over, I will easily find it. Should it be resolved at 4:16 a.m. one sleepless night, it will swiftly be replaced with something new. I am, alas, a worrier.

Through practice, I've become pretty good at it. I can toggle efficiently among a range of potential threats, even as I blanch or shudder at various imagined catastrophes: the satanic undertow out of nowhere. The chairlift that inexplicably derails. The child who tumbles down the stairs, me careening just a moment too late after. We won't even mention air travel.

And of course there's the old standby, something most of us

have pictured at one point or another: The house on fire. Everything bursting into flames. Only moments to decide what to save beyond children, spouse, small animals. Do I grab the birth certificates, the tax backup, the passports—if only to spare myself the paperwork? Do I go with the valuable or with the irreplaceable? My grandmother's ring, my poorly collected letters, the computer in case the cloud evaporates?

I wouldn't bother with any of those things. In my heart, I know that were everything burning to ashes at my feet, I'd leave behind the laptop and the photo albums and even, forgive me, my children's artwork, because there is one object I'd need to rescue above all else—my true precious, Bob.

Bob isn't a pet or a teddy bear, though he does hold sentimental value and has been with me since my school days. Unimaginatively abbreviated, BOB is my Book of Books, a bound record of everything I've read or didn't quite finish reading since the summer of 1988, my junior year in high school. It's my way of keeping track. Because if I didn't write it all down, I worry (naturally), I would forget it.

He's nothing fancy, this Book of Books of mine. He isn't hand woven by artisanal craftsmen from a Himalayan village or decoratively embossed. No, he is factory-made, gray and plain, with a charcoal binding and white unlined paper, an inelegant relic from the days before bookstores stocked Moleskine notebooks, before blogging and scrapbooking and "journaling" as a verb. Within his covers lies a running account of authors and titles, which I dutifully enter upon the completion of every book I read. After around twenty books or so, when I remember to put it there, a vague date breaks up the catalog.

I first wrote about Bob, with no small amount of trepidation, in an essay for the *New York Times Book Review* in 2012. Further exposing myself, I allowed the text to be accompanied by a photograph of Bob's first page, displaying to millions of strangers my early stabs at depth and intellectualism, fleeting girlish obsessions, deliberately obscure annotations, and all. I had revealed my inner life in a very public way, but at least, I reasoned, I'd done so in a safe place, among fellow readers. As soon as the *Book Review*'s art director scanned in the appropriate page, I recovered Bob from the seventh-floor art department and spirited him safely back home. He hasn't left since.

My Book of Books is still a private place. It's not a traditional diary, to be sure. It's about me, and yet it isn't about me. It's impersonal and yet deeply personal. And in my case, it has worked better than a "real" diary, that basic prerequisite for anyone who fancies herself a future writer. Bob has lasted a lot longer than any of my abandoned teenage journals—I write in it still—and here's why: diaries contained all kinds of things I wanted to forget—unrequited crushes and falling-outs with friends and angsting over college admissions. Bob contains things I wanted to remember: what I was reading when all that happened.

Now in his middle age, Bob offers immediate access to where I've been, psychologically and geographically, at any given moment in my life. How I decided on a certain book. What I'd read previously that had either put me in the mood for more of the same or driven me toward something different. Was I in a Civil War stage or up for a good spy novel? Had I read the author previously and, if so, when? Why had I left him and what drew me back? Bob may not always seal into memory the identities of individual characters—much of that is still lost in the cavern—but he does tell me more about *my* character.

———

Each entry conjures a memory that may have otherwise gotten lost or blurred with time. Opening Bob, I remember lying in a dormitory in Mauriac, an unspectacular hamlet in central France where I was installed on an American Field Service program, when I wrote my first entry: *The Trial*, fittingly, an unfinished work. This summons a flood of attendant recollections: seeing Baryshnikov perform in *Metamorphosis*, on Broadway, which led me to the paperback Kafka I packed with me that summer—an entire swath of Sturm und Drang adolescence reemerges from the fog of those other things I'd rather forget.

The immediacy of these recollections often startles me. Whereas old diaries later read like transcribed dreams—Who wrote that? Was it really *me* who got so worked up/wanted that guy/obsessed about X?—book titles easily and accurately manage to evoke an earlier state of mind. *Yes*, I think, reading over the entries: I remember that. I remember that book jacket, that edition, the feel of those pages. For a girl who often felt like she lived more in the cozy world of books than in the unforgiving world of the playground, a book of books was the richest journal imaginable; it showed a version of myself I recognized and felt represented me.

Over the years, Bob has become an even more personal record than a diary might have been, not about my quotidian existence but about what lay at its foundations—what drove my interests and shaped my ideas. There's where I was physically, sitting in the cat-wallpapered room I'd ambitiously decorated in the second grade or at a leftover table in the high school cafeteria—and then there was where I lived in my mind, surrounded by my chosen people, conversing with aplomb in carefully appointed drawing rooms or roaming in picturesque fashion across windswept English landscapes.

Today my life is engulfed in books. Built-in shelves line my bedroom, adjacent to my Japanese platform bed, purchased for its capacious rim, the better to hold those books that must be immediately accessible. Yet still they pile on my nightstand, and the grid of shelves continues in floor-to-ceiling formation across the wall, stampeding over the doorway in disorderly fashion, political memoirs mixed in with literary essays, Victorian novels fighting for space with narrative adventure, the Penguin classics never standing together in a gracious row no matter how hard I try to impose order. The books compete for attention, assembling on the shelf above the sofa on the other side of the room, where they descend by the window, staring back at me. As I lie in bed with another book, they lie in wait.

The books don't stop there. They gather on a coffee table in front of that sofa, and in my home office, where they mount according to intended destination—books to donate to my kids' school, books to give to the local library, books meant for my husband, my mother, my in-laws in California, one of my three children. They fill up totebags that loiter by the staircase, ready to be hauled onto the train, commuting back and forth, some making the return trip, others staying on.

In my office at the *New York Times Book Review*, they are greeted by like-minded company. Books of interest, books with a purpose, books that are there for a reason. A shelf in front of my desk contains books I may want to refer to someday, by authors who've piqued my interest, or who are worth considering as potential reviewers for our pages, or whose work has already been

MY LIFE WITH BOB

praised. Books to be read, books to be read, books to be read. Books that may one day make their way into Bob.

When I come home and look back through my Book of Books I see a personal narrative I didn't recognize at the time. I went from escaping into books to extracting things from them, from being inspired by books to trying to do things that inspired me—many of which I first encountered in stories. I went from wishing I were like a character in books to being a character in my books. I went from reading books to wrestling with them to writing them, all the while still learning from what I read.

The prospect of losing Bob has become more vexing as he and I have gotten older. I no longer take him on trips. Now he stays safely at home and I tend to his pages as soon as I unpack, logging in the books read on planes and trains and between meetings. With each entry, I grow more guarded about his contents. I feel as protective of Bob as I do of myself.

Though I thought he'd have long been filled by now and succeeded by a second book, there is still only one of him. He is less than half full, almost exactly mirroring my place in expected life span. He still has so much work to do, so many pages to fill. Yet after nearly three decades, Bob is showing his age. I am sometimes careless with him, which I then feel guilty about. A decade ago I unthinkingly repeated a full one-hundred sequence in error; much scratching out followed. I write entries hurriedly, while standing up, underlining the titles in wavy, discordant lines. His pages betray a certain amount of misuse. At some point, I spilled coffee on him; the cover is mottled and discolored, the binding has split, one corner is woody and bare. He sits on a special shelf, right over my desk, the anonymity of his unappealingly frayed spine ensuring our privacy.

Without Bob, something feels worryingly missing—missing from my life and from the accounting of my life. A book is somehow not quite read, and my own story doesn't quite make sense, the two inextricably linked. I don't know where I'd be without Bob and where I'd have been if he hadn't been there. Bob may be a record of other people's stories, but he's mine. If there's any book that tells me my own story, it's this one.

CHAPTER I

Brave New World

You Shouldn't Be Reading That

When you're a child, reading is full of rules. Books that are appropriate and books that are not, books that grown-ups will smile at you approvingly for cradling in your arms and those that will cause grimaces when they spy you tearing through their pages. There are books you're not supposed to be reading, at least not just yet. There is a time and a place.

But for me it felt like there was never enough time, and the place was elusive. Bringing a book of your own to school was a no-no, and not to recess either, where you were supposed to be getting balls thrown at your head. Carrying a book was practically against the law at summer camp, where downtime was for forced mass song. Children were meant to be running around, engaged in active, healthy play with other hardy boys and girls.

I hated running around.

Before every elementary school classroom had a "Drop Everything and Read" period, before parents and educators agonized more about children being glued to Call of Duty or getting sucked into the vortex of the Internet, reading as a childhood activity was not always revered. Maybe it was in some families, in some towns, in some magical places that seemed to exist only in stories, but not where I was. Nobody trotted out the kid who read all the time as someone to be admired like the ones who did tennis and ballet and other feats requiring basic coordination.

While those other kids pursued their after-school activities in earnest, I failed at art, gymnastics, ice skating, soccer, and ballet with a lethal mix of inability, fear, and boredom. Coerced into any group endeavor, I wished I could just be home already. Rainy days were a godsend because you could curl up on a sofa without being banished into the outdoors with an ominous "Go play outside."

Well into adulthood, I would chastise myself over not settling on a hobby—knitting or yoga or swing dancing or crosswords—and just reading instead. The default position. Everyone else had a passion; where was mine? How much happier I would have been to know that reading was itself a passion. Nobody treated it that way, and it didn't occur to me to think otherwise.

People laugh today at Roald Dahl's idea that Matilda's father would scream at his daughter to watch TV rather than slink off with a book, but there is a tiny sliver of truth to the satire, where, on the dark side of seventies benign neglect, parents didn't run around boasting "She's such a reader!" or try to bribe their kids into summer reading. You were supposed to be well rounded, not bookish. Reading too much hurt your eyes and made you need glasses. So did reading by poor light. My own bedside lamp, my mother pointed out, got especially hot and was a fire hazard. Reading in cars made you throw up. Squinting at too-small letters left you blind.

There was a shiftiness to kids who secreted themselves in a corner to read God knows what instead of what they should have been doing. Reading when you were supposed to be raking the leaves, reading when you were supposed to be sleeping, reading when you were supposed to be making the bed, not lying in it. I did everything I could to read my way out of doing anything else. It was the one thing I was good at.

Social skills were not my forte. I was shy as a child, and if my nose was in a book, nobody had to know about this failing. Anything to have fewer adults declare loudly right in front of me, "Oh, she's *shy*! Look at her hiding—that's okay. I didn't realize she was *shy*," as if they'd found out I lacked a key mental faculty. At school, I walked around in a state of perpetual embarrassment, certain others could sniff out something different about me. Any second I might trip and fall in front of everyone or find a peanut butter smear on my pants that had been there since lunch period. Or I might accidentally sit at the wrong table, setting off some kind of social distress signal that every other kid but me could hear.

Afraid of being left out or singled out, I turned myself into an independent agent, only lightly associated with others. I read alone, I biked alone, I fed the ducks across the street alone, and I played with my cat alone. I was the only girl among seven brothers, and for the most part our interests did not align. "You must have been so spoiled, so cared for!" people say when they learn about my solitary femaleness; nothing could have been further from reality. Anytime I exhibited the merest sign of girl-ishness it was mocked into oblivion; I grew resentful of any "privilege" that marked me apart. Whenever my brothers were paired off into bedrooms, I felt exiled; I could hear them whisper-ing among themselves through thin walls. At any moment, one of them might wrestle me to the ground, pin me down, and let a gob of saliva dangle threateningly over my face.

My parents divorced when I was three or four (nobody seems to remember exactly), and my father had moved to a series of small rentals on the Upper West Side and then into his girl-friend's rent-stabilized middle-income apartment on Columbus Avenue with her two sons. My mother remarried when I was seven, and we moved to an ancient house in a new town with her new husband and his three much older sons. Though her new husband was retired, my mother worked long hours juggling multiple jobs, commuting into the city, where she was an adver-tising copywriter; then she worked into the night freelance edit-ing a series of trade magazines. My brothers and I largely fended for ourselves, walking to school and returning home on our own. Arguments were to be "worked out" among ourselves. This usually meant threats, slammed doors, and occasional outbursts of violence. I tended to miss when I kicked.

Families seemed better inside books; in *All-of-a-Kind Family* and *Little Women*, there were sisters. (All I had was my cousin Kirsten, three years younger and always living somewhere far away—Florida, Germany, Colorado Springs.) Families in books were large and friendly; siblings hugged one another spontane-ously and ate scrumptious holiday meals around a table. Nobody sat stonily through servings of boiled spinach and baked potatoes. One day, I resolved, I would have a family like *that*.

I had the misfortune of being an exceptionally healthy child, never having an infection or vomiting, with only one or two fevers to show for my entire school career. How I longed to be ill so I could stay home and read. No such luck. My mom could spot a faker and had little patience for anything that wasn't a sky-high fever. It was a blow to discover that the trick that worked in books—putting a thermometer by the lightbulb—didn't work in real life.

Reading time became *my* time and place, another dimension where events operated by my own set of rules. Nobody else needed to know when you snuck off with your Sweet Valley Highs whether you were a Jessica who wished she were an Elizabeth or vice versa. What you read revealed what you cared about and feared, what you hoped for because you didn't have it, what questions you wanted answered without publicly unmasking your ignorance. I guarded this information fiercely.

Like W. H. Auden, who once wrote, "Occasionally, I come across a book which I feel has been written especially for me and for me only," I considered certain books mine, and the idea that other people liked them and thought of them as theirs felt like an intrusion. ("Like a jealous lover, I don't want anybody else to hear of it"—Auden, again.) I wanted to be the only one who knew about a book or at least to be the first one there.

In fourth grade, reading *Forever* felt like breaking the law with every turn of the page. Just acknowledging Judy Blume's existence, with her frank acknowledgment of tweenish emotions, filled me with shame. That the procuring of such intimate books had to be public was horrifying especially because I cared enormously what the library staff thought of me. I liked to imagine the clerk surveying my outgoing stack with admiration and approval. *Look at that wise little girl*, he was meant to think. *She's one of us.* When I checked out the Blumes, I'd wait until the coast was clear, staring resolutely away from the clerk like a thirteen-year-old buying Tampax, hoping he wouldn't connect me with that other sage girl who read Louisa May Alcott.

I was certain I'd lose their respect entirely if they caught me when, following the gateway drug of Judy Blume, I progressed to Paula Danziger and Norma Klein, explicit and positively dirty. That there were books I *knew* were inappropriate, and that I wanted to read them anyway, was obviously a personality flaw. The climax of exploitative teenage lit was, of course, V. C. Andrews's scintillating incest series that began with *Flowers in the Attic*, but those I got at Barnes & Noble. I wasn't prepared to risk *everything*.

Eventually, having worn out the children's floor, I ventured upstairs toward the grown-up library. On a kind of purgatorial mezzanine stood three rotating racks filled with what then passed as young adult fiction. Most were romances, including Sweet Dreams.

Clearly there was something disgraceful about the Sweet Dreams series. With titles like *P.S. I Love You* and *The Popularity Plan*, they were displayed unforgivingly in a wide-open space where grown-ups could see exactly what you were doing. I would dash up and quickly spin the rack, eyes scanning expertly for heretofore undiscovered volumes. The covers featured photographs of before-they-were-famous teenage actresses gazing soulfully. A gangly sixth grader with a greasy center part, I didn't look anything like those cover girls, and I certainly didn't know romance. I had to read every single one.

But I could easily cross the line into places that still felt decidedly off-limits, even to me. Once, at Barnes & Noble, I chose a novel with the naked back of a silhouetted female torso on its cover, decades before such images became the tired trope of "women's fiction." It looked daring, but not dangerous; I had no idea what it was about. When I got home and started to read, I quickly realized I'd entered uncharted territory for a ten-year-old kid in 1980s Long Island. What was this word "lesbian"? If I read the book and was found out, it was certain there would be terrible repercussions.

Better to just turn myself in. My mom was sitting in the living room when I approached in a sweat, book upside down as if to mask its incendiary contents.

"I don't think this is for me," I said, handing it over with instant relief. My mother took the book away wordlessly, and we never spoke of it again.

"The trouble with books," Jeanette Winterson's mother once admonished her, "is that you don't know what's in them until it's too late." This is precisely right. We might read about things we weren't supposed to, find out what adults didn't want us to discover. But this wasn't altogether bad. Books, I soon realized, were a way to acquire illicit knowledge, a key to adulthood that otherwise remained hidden, whether you were entirely ready or not. I'd been a fool to relinquish that power.

Books are how cautious kids get to experience a kind of secondhand rebellion, a safe way to go off the rails. While for the most part I sought out any book bearing the golden seal of the Newbery Medal, safe and "good" books, perhaps in part to balance that as I got older, I was drawn to the troublemakers— the Edie Sedgwicks and Jim Morrisons and Marilyn Monroes. Soon, I had to get my hands on anything remotely "countercultural,"

Lady Chatterley's Lover, Madame Bovary, and what I thought of as "bad boy" books—the Beats, cult favorites, any title that had somewhere at some point been banned.

Not all these books were as fun as expected. I was bored by *Zen and the Art of Motorcycle Maintenance* and hated *On the Road*, and I hated *The Catcher in the Rye* even more. Their heroes seemed more like antiheroes; fundamentally eager to please, I wasn't open to characters who thumbed their noses at the authorities. I felt compelled to read them nonetheless and have felt equally disinclined to return to them since. But the more downtrodden characters, I positively adored. Anyone who was a heroin addict or knew a heroin addict or wrote about another heroin addict was good enough for me. Accounts of dead drug-addicted celebrities constituted their own lush genre, the more sordid the behavior and devastating the downfall, the better. I felt sorry for them, and this emotional largesse made me feel better about me.

This made the forceful removal of the next "inappropriate" book devastating. It was the early eighties. *Saturday Night Live* was the height of cool. It didn't matter that I'd never actually stayed up late enough for the TV show because there was a book, *Wired*, Bob Woodward's bestselling biography of John Belushi. *Wired* had been featured on magazine covers, which meant it was important. When my mother caught me with a copy—and only on the opening chapter!—she swiped it. No amount of tears would overturn her decision.

The truth is she had nothing to fear. Reading about bad guys scared the hell out of me, reinforcing the line between us. In real life, nothing about the rebels and willful misfits was remotely appealing. Listening to Holden Caulfield moan and groan, I couldn't help but think, *What a jerk*. What did he have to complain about, with his privileged life and his private school and his afternoons wandering unsupervised around Manhattan?

My attraction to the dark side may have been that it allowed me to explore the forbidden from a safe distance, helping me draw distinctions between the kind of person I wanted to be and what I wanted to avoid. When I grim-mindedly chose to read *Brave New World*, along with *1984* and *A Clockwork Orange*, for my honors thesis in high school, it was my way of proving I was grown-up enough to make these choices.

In the World State of Aldous Huxley's *Brave New World*, people are not allowed to spend time by themselves; leisure time is to be spent thoughtlessly in benign group activity. Serious literature is banned and children are taught to stay in their place through targeted subconscious messages. Not surprisingly, *Brave New World* is one of the most frequently banned books in America, due to its "subversive" content. *Brave New World* was not for children, and that's partly what made it irresistible.

The title comes from Shakespeare's play *The Tempest*:

> O wonder!
> How many godly creatures are there here!
> How beauteous mankind is! O brave new world,
> That has such people in't.

This was intended ironically, by Shakespeare and by Huxley, who proposed that, in lieu of beauteous mankind serving the greater interest, the world was full of selfish and nefarious people out to advance themselves. But for me, *Brave New World* held another, altogether different meaning. Books were my brave new world, my portal into the forbidden adult world, one that I could approach in my own vicarious way, drawing my own conclusions.

What a thrill it was to read beyond your means, asserting yourself through the books you chose, breaking the rules just slightly but in a way that helped define your own rules. As I got older, it began to dawn on me that nobody really knew or cared what I did inside a book, or why I was there. The clerks at the library weren't actually monitoring my activity. I stopped feeling embarrassed about my selections and became more confident about my ability to choose what I wanted. I even began to feel proud of those choices and, I liked to think, fairly sophisticated in my judgment. (I wasn't always right about this.) The brave new world outside might have been intimidating, but I could travel there surreptitiously inside a book, and if I played it right I would never get in trouble.

CHAPTER 2

Slaves of New York

The Literary Life

Children are notoriously literal readers, and I was no exception. Books, I believed, contained the entire truth about everything, and if you could just read every book or even a good chunk of the Truly Important Ones, you would know what you needed to know about real life. And you could be a part of it.

Naturally, I got a lot of things wrong. When I was eleven, I told my mother quite adamantly that Norma Klein wrote the classic 1939 folk song "You Are My Sunshine," because it had appeared in one of her teen-weepy novels, the song a husband lovingly sang to his dying wife. "I really don't think so," my mother replied, but what did she know? I'd read it that way so it had to be true.

All books, to my mind, were essentially guidebooks. I sucked them up the way Martha the dog slurps alphabet soup in *Martha*

Speaks and learns how to talk. I was precisely what Hermann Hesse once called a "naïve reader," consuming books as one consumes food, swallowing them whole. "This kind of reader is not related to a book as one person is to another but rather as a horse to his manager or perhaps as a horse to his driver: the book leads, the reader follows," Hesse explained. "The substance is taken objectively, accepted as reality." Exactly. And what was wrong with that?

Reading could instruct you on how to live, and not only that—it could teach you how to live the smartest, coolest, most urbane life imaginable, which meant nobody would ever be able to tell how silly and ignorant and suburban you once were. Books about older, wiser, and all-around better people would prepare you for anything that happened outside of books. They would make it clear how to act and how to react.

I didn't question, I didn't ponder, I didn't criticize. I merely absorbed, down to the word. Books were where I picked up my vocabulary, extracting the words I needed to get around. Germaine Greer recalls how she would adopt a word from a given book, using it "for a whole day until I got the feel of it, 'fetch' or 'directly' or 'capital' or 'coaxing' or 'melancholy.'" I made lists of aspirational words. Like Greer, I wanted to think and speak the way writing did. This, alas, had the unfortunate effect of making me sound awkward and pretentious, precisely like the poorly socialized kid I was.

Having learned how to speak more from what I read than from what I heard, I excelled at mispronunciation. Mildred became "Mild Red," like a soft shade of scarlet, which seemed rather pretty. I was always horrified to be corrected, and occasionally insisted my way was the right one even in the face of decisive evidence to the contrary. I did not, like many other readers I know, take to saying "mih-zled" in place of misled, but I nonetheless repeatedly embarrassed myself, feeling exposed as a fraud when someone pointed out that "vogue" was not, in fact, pronounced "voe-goo." (Years later, the literary critic Liesl Schillinger would dub these "mumblenyms"—words mispronounced by heavy readers who'd encountered them only on the page.)

It was important to me to feel book smart, because my future depended on it. Once I'd gleaned the right information, I could decide which books were part of my desired world and will myself into them. I could imagine leaving behind where I was physically (grayish-pink bedroom, cat wallpaper, Long Island), stepping through a hardcover door, and venturing "out there."

Out there, in stories, was the City I knew from Divorced Dad weekends at my father's apartment on the Upper West Side, a place that felt like a parallel Almost Existence, a place where I might have lived had the divorce played out differently, a place where I may have felt more at home. As it was, I was a part-time and therefore inauthentic resident, which made any book that smelled at all of Manhattan deeply alluring. Mine but not mine. Tell-alls about downtown bohemians, books by theater types, gritty street stories—this was the life I wanted, full of sophisticated people, arty events, sparkling conversation that was all about words, spoken by people who knew.

Andy Warhol was my literary guide. Any book about or endorsed by Andy Warhol, still alive and ineffably cool, roaming coolly around midtown, I had to get my hands on. One afternoon in the city, I was thunderstruck to spot Warhol himself, oohing over a shelf of impulse buys in the extremely hip and expensive store Fiorucci. Here was a veritable City Celebrity and obvious literary authority, in real life, in *my* life. I shadowed him for forty-five minutes, prolonging the moment of Art Become Real. He picked up trinket after trinket. He didn't buy anything.

My best friend, Ericka, and I may have been the only teenagers in America who appointment-viewed Warhol's short-lived MTV program, *Andy Warhol's 15 Minutes*, which we religiously recorded on the VCR, practically taking notes. As far as we were concerned, Warhol and his circle had the ultimate say, perhaps along with *Spy* magazine, on what we construed as literature of the moment. Anyone who appeared on Warhol's TV show and had a book, I read it. Bret Easton Ellis, *Less Than Zero*. Jay McInerney, *Bright Lights, Big City*. Sandra Bernhard's *Confessions of a Pretty Lady*, with its scandalous line in which Bernhard casually confessed to picking her nose while walking down the street. For someone who felt self-conscious walking down the street just trying to appear normal, Bernhard's audacity dazzled.

Ever since Ericka and I had met in Girl Scouts in second grade, we'd shared a propensity for fantasy. In fourth grade, we constructed an elaborate world called Oopleepia; this planet was located in the tree house outside my father's rental house upstate and ruled by the great god Oopleep. Ericka was an alien named Eep and I was Oop. Years later, I confessed that I'd always been jealous that she'd had the cuter name. "You had the cuter name," she replied. We were always slightly competitive.

Naturally, our fantasies evolved as we got older, ditched Girl Scouts, and ran with and then away from a bad crowd, making our way through the gross injustice of junior high school, remaining best friends all the while. By the time we graduated from eighth grade, most of our imaginary life revolved around downtown lit and the New Wave music we deemed forward-thinking, a mix tape of one-hit wonders that also made room for perennial heartthrobs Sting and Duran Duran. Ericka's mother worked at *Billboard*, her uncle was the lead singer of a seventies rock group, my stepbrother played in a band—all this translated into assorted brushes with fame: backstage passes to teenybop concerts like 'Til Tuesday at the old Ritz, INXS at the Meadowlands, Simple Minds at the Beacon Theatre. We snuck into the Limelight and Nell's, me covering my braces with one hand. We even managed to speak to Simon Le Bon on the phone, a conversation during which one of us—name redacted—blurted out, "Is John Taylor getting married?" The apotheosis was snagging a bit part dancing in the background of a Nile Rodgers video, my colossal hair threatening to blot out all else on-screen.

We may not have gotten ourselves married off to Sting or Simon Le Bon, but we considered them part of our lives, earning us cultural passports out of the high school world where we were ignored by the popular girls in their capacious Champion sweatshirts (overpriced, essential) and Silver City Pink lipstick. We could dip into the milieu we read about in *Spy* magazine as long as nobody else (our parents) knew about it. If only the other kids at school could know.

Tristate-area alumni know how terrible it is to be merely New York–ish when, inside, you feel like a New Yorker. The City was only forty minutes away and yet so far from the minds of my classmates. How could you not want to at least read about it?

Something had to be done, and luckily, someone had made the senseless error of putting me in a leadership position in a key high school organization. The Human Relations Committee sounds like a nefarious political lobby but was actually an extracurricular activity that had some kind of ineffable touchy-feely purpose. The nature of this purpose remained elusive to me and my coleaders, two attractive and more socially adept classmates; I had an unrequited crush on the arty one and spent copious amounts of time vacillating wildly between the conviction that he knew all about my crush and the certainty that he had no clue about my true feelings. He was either totally mortified to even be liked by me or secretly in love with me too. I could never be sure. What did I know about human relations?

And what *was* Human Relations? How had we landed these roles? Did we even have a faculty advisor? Unclear. As best I understood it, we were to convene a handpicked sample of twenty-five students every month from each stratum of high school society for a day of interclique bonding at the local public library. It was like *The Breakfast Club*, but without Judd Nelson and not a movie.

In a quixotic effort to make my high school classmates more book—and Manhattan—aware and because we met in the library, which was my turf (also to impress the arty one), I decided one of the group's activities would be a read-aloud. I chose the reading, and it was always the same: *Slaves of New York*.

Tama Janowitz had recently published the book, her debut collection of stories, with a blurb on the back from Andy Warhol that said, "Great! Sizzling! Wow!" Janowitz, with her bushel of black hair, wide apple cheeks, and tiny beak of a nose, had read parts of the book aloud on *Andy Warhol's 15 Minutes* with great panache, in a mocking, deadpan voice dripping with insouciance. I taped the episode and watched it over and over, studying her delivery. She was the coolest author I'd ever seen and she deserved a wider audience. She would also prove to my audience that I was cool just for reading her.

Because oversight of the HRC was minimal to nonexistent,

I was able to force my group of twenty-five peers each month into a circle and read to them from Janowitz's "Case History N4: Fred," aping her unassailable nonchalance, her unforced charm, her indifference to resolved endings. She didn't care what anyone thought and, dammit, I'd pretend I didn't either.

The story had a killer opening: "Fred had a problem: he liked to approach strange girls on the street and offer to take them shopping at Tiffany's." As I read, I watched everyone's face to make sure they were registering the appropriate level of appreciation. The story was only three pages long; even so, I made a few judicious cuts. My classmates didn't need to know he was an out-of-work musician who lived near the Williamsburg Bridge, for example. But there were key parts, like this exchange:

"To his surprise, he found himself saying, 'Listen, I like your linear definition. I was wondering—just for the hell of it—would you let me take you shopping at Tiffany's? It would give me a great deal of pleasure, and naturally I wouldn't expect payment of any kind.'

"The girl looked at him and said, 'Buzz off.' "

That was it. End of activity. There was no discussion of the story, of what it meant, of its relevance, of why I'd decided to read it to a bunch of kids from school. I conducted the reading like a sermon. Why a teacher or librarian didn't question this practice I have never understood. In my mind, I was performing a service: *Here is what you need to know.* And moreover, *This is what I wish you knew about me. Or knew that I know.*

It was my inchoate way of declaring to the rest of my high school classmates where I stood. Ericka and I and a few other friends didn't fit neatly into any one group. We were more like floaters, and even among the floaters, I didn't have any defining characteristic; there was no part for me in the John Hughes lineup. Everyone else had some kind of identity—the lacrosse player, the theater person, the hot arty guy, the popular one, the popular one who's also a good student—part of me wanted to stake out mine: book person.

A book person was someone who knew things other kids didn't. She knew about culture and art, about literary alliances and feuds, about writers who had made it, writers who were on the cusp, and writers who had fallen out of favor. She knew which books mattered.

A book person had her own sources and understood the use of imagination. By declaring yourself a book person, you could make your fellow students aware that you were privy to another dimension of the world, and so the slights in their world—not having a boyfriend or not getting invited to a party or not having the right sweatshirt or not achieving a certain rank in the suburban hierarchy—didn't matter. You were part of something else.

I had not yet made the transition from thinking that everything in a book was true and good to being a discriminating or even a mildly skeptical reader. I didn't question whether the urban life depicted in the books I deemed sophisticated and desirable was in fact a happy one, with depth or consequence. Instead, I hoovered it all up into the vacuum of my mind. I felt ahead of the game, convinced that if only I read enough books, I would have everything I needed for the life I wanted, both aware and unaware of how little I really knew.

CHAPTER 3

The Trial

A Book with No Ending

I was supposed to be asleep. Instead I was reading *The Trial* on the sly, camped out in a dorm bed in rural France, hiding my book under the covers like a forbidden telephone after hours. I turned the pages quickly but quietly, desperate to know the ending but for nobody to know I was even awake. I was missing all my classes and let everyone think I was sick, but the truth was I had jet lag and a hangover. I was seventeen, this was my first time abroad, and it turned out I was a big baby when it came to switching time zones.

Falling in with Sigrid, a girl as hard-edged as her name, during the predeparture orientation on Long Island had not been helpful. We were supposed to be preparing for our impending summer abroad, a cultural immersion program run by the American Field Service, which would begin with a month of classes and culminate in a monthlong homestay with a French family. Instead, we'd ditched the prep schedule to "party" in an abandoned college lounge.

Sigrid has to mean "up to no good" in some language. Flown in from one suburban wasteland or another, she had forced yellow hair, pointed features, and an inborn smirk; if it had been the aughts and not the eighties, she would have had multiple piercings and at least one Sanskrit tattoo. After several hours of drinking smuggled alcohol, she whipped out a joint, which she sprinkled with white powder from a small vial. Cocaine! Sigrid reeled in another blonde, who partook with gusto. This second girl looked like Marilyn Monroe, and we shellacked her in Maybelline to accentuate the resemblance, then took dozens of Polaroid pictures of ourselves, mostly the second blonde, who struck a series of half-lidded poses. In the course of forty-eight hours, we used most of the film intended to document our respective summers abroad.

I nearly left my camera behind. I nearly missed the plane. I almost wished I had missed the plane, because it hit a patch of rough air over the Atlantic and dipped its way to Europe in bell-curved swoops. I'd never been on an overseas flight and was petrified. By the time we got to France, I felt more dead than alive. I have no recollection of the journey out of Paris, other than that it took place under a sour pall of resentment at being cheated out of the most important part of the country. A lucky batch of students got to stay in the Île de France area while the rest of us splintered off into various corners of the country. Somehow, my group made its way to the tiny backwater of Mauriac, a place so lost in the center of France that every French person I've met subsequently has furrowed their brow in confusion when I named the location of my July 1988 sojourn: *"Où?! C'est dans quel département? Mais c'est n'importe où!,"* which translates roughly into "Where the hell is that?"

Even a parochial American adolescent could tell that Mauriac was up somewhere in France's armpit. I had finally gotten "out there"—outside my books and my town and into a life that could possibly *be* a story instead of just a life reading about other people's stories—and yet I was still nowhere, in the kind of charmless spot even Peter Mayle couldn't make appealing. Why, of all corners of France, from its alpine heights to its Mediterranean beaches to its lavender-scented hills to its chic metropolises, had I been sent to wretched Mauriac, a down-on-its-heels town with one *hypermarché* and a dwindling population of four thousand? A place known primarily for its cheese, which frankly isn't a mark of distinction in rural France. A place founded as if in error, when the daughter of a Frankish king had a vision of the Virgin Mary carrying the baby Jesus and accompanied by Saint Peter, which led her to build a chapel by a small stream. She'd clearly been deluded onto this path to nowhere. Everything about this place was wrong and I, peevish teenage ingrate, felt wronged, too.

I was epically hungover and thoroughly jet-lagged, and like a child angrily scratching at a poison ivy rash to make it go away, I kept making it worse. I refused to enter my new time zone and slept instead, waking up at odd hours and reading, reading, reading.

Kafka's opening line in *The Trial* seemed to carry a personal message, as it surely has for many readers feeling surly with the world: "Someone must have been telling lies about Joseph K., for without having done anything wrong he was arrested one fine morning." Exactly right. I, too, was being unfairly punished.

Fine, I'd been a bad kid, skipping out on orientation, but was that so disgraceful I had to be stuck in a town where acid-washed jeans were still the height of fashion? (Sigrid was long gone, swept off to some doubtless more sophisticated province where she was probably shooting up French heroin.)

The other kids in my unit surely hated me already. What kind of jerk has the audacity to blow off an entire transatlantic orientation program? Why come to France if you aren't going to participate? Who's so fancy or neurasthenic she can't bother getting out of bed for thirty-six hours?

It felt appropriate then that I was reading *The Trial*, a tale of injustice if ever there was one. I, too, was the victim of a cruel and arbitrary yet somehow preordained fate. All my seventeen years, I'd never gotten to travel, a tragedy rubbed in by classmates from the wealthier parts of town, kids who seemed to fly off to Club Med every winter break, their peeled noses a mark of status upon return. My family, an unwieldy blend of stepfamilies totaling eight kids, never went on vacation. We didn't have the money, there were too many of us, and not enough of us got along.

Instead, we had sporadic visits to indifferent grandparents in Florida and Virginia and long weekends of East Coast skiing, during which my brothers paired up with my city stepbrothers and dumped me in the singles line, yet another instance in which being the only girl was a strike against me. Once they abandoned me at Killington, where I descended the wrong slope of the mountain and cried into a mound of dirty snow until an announcement over the resort's loudspeakers summoned me to return. Other kids at school seemed to go to Italy or even Disney World. I'd been to Disney World once, back when you had to pay per ride and so I got to choose exactly one (It's a Small World, no less); we ate warm Saran-wrapped sandwiches that we brought with us because eating out was "a fortune"—don't even think about asking for a Mickey Mouse–shaped balloon. I was too busy feeling deprived to realize that this was still in fact rather privileged.

And now, once again, my parents' stinginess had ruined things; if only I'd been allowed to do the more upscale Experiment in International Living program rather than the cut-rate AFS. Of course I'd ended up tired and friendless in a lost patch of barely French France.

I was adolescence incarnate. And like many adolescents full of adolescent feelings, I wanted to commemorate my angst and fury the way adolescents do: in a diary. I had brought a blank book with me to France, purchased at a local stationery store for its forbidding charcoal exterior and wide-open unlined pages. This diary, I'd decided from the get-go, would be different from all my previous diaries, each of which I'd pushed aside in dismay after a few months of erratic entries.

Those diaries were hellish. For the most part, I'd open them only when I'd sunk to a true low, and as a last and loathsome resort. I wrote when I found out that Katie had slept over Ingrid's house after she'd said no to sleeping over mine. I wrote when Ingrid and Wendy played a prank by using the then new conference call function to simultaneously get me and a stranger on the phone together, each of us thinking the other had initiated the call, and then cackle inaudibly at our mutual confusion. I wrote when every single one of my silent, humiliating crushes in junior high went unnoticed or ignored, each awful in its own way—and, in the aggregate, devastating. I wrote when I was angry, I wrote when I was rejected, I wrote when I felt fat-thighed or uncoordinated or especially pimple-ridden.

On occasion, I'd pick up an old diary, hoping to see flashes of Anne Frank or at least a Judy Blume character, some flicker of talent or originality of thought. I found nothing of the sort. Instead, revisiting past entries became an exercise in regret, a resurrection of dormant upset and humiliation, all of it in flustered prose full of delusional self-promises and fleeting gusts of determination, ink swelling where I'd leaned heavily on the pen as I wrote: "I'm *never* calling Wendy again!" "Could it be possible he likes me, too, but is too proud to admit it?" "I didn't want to go to that stupid beach party, anyway."

Not surprisingly, these diaries did not make for a pleasant or rewarding reading experience. No way was I going to vomit my insecurities and insults into another one, not on my first trip abroad, not the summer before my senior year, not so close to my impending collegiate escape. No. This diary would be about something better than me, or rather about the better part of me, the imagined part, and yet the real part. This book would be about my books.

One morning, when nobody else was in the dormitory, after I finished the last pages of *The Trial* and put it on the shelf over my bed, I pulled down the new diary and a pen. Across the top of the first page, I wrote my name in black ink and, directly below, "Book Journal." Then I flipped the page and began my Book of Books. Neatly across the top, I wrote in underlined columns: "Date," "Author," "Title." And I marked down my first entry: "July/August 1988, Kafka, *The Trial.*" Later, I would add an asterisk next to Kafka's name and the names of all the other books I read that summer. This symbol I gave to books that were fun reading, *my* books. Books for school, which dominated during that period of my life, would go unmarked; they were the default. (This designation later reversed, then disappeared altogether.)

I didn't tell anyone else at AFS about my new diary; like my hangover and the rudimentary state of my French and *The Trial* under my covers, it was my secret. My book of books. My Bob.

Eventually, I made a few friends, the kind one now sees scroll by on Facebook, though none of them close enough to tell about Bob. As it happens, the closest friend I made in France wasn't even there. Reading a letter over the shoulder of a fellow AFS student named Susie, I met someone for the first time purely through writing. He was sharp, opinionated, and very, very funny. He wrote far better than anyone I knew spoke, not just getting the words out but choosing them with consideration before committing them to the page.

"Who wrote this?" I asked Susie when I got to the end of the letter, which read as if it had been written as much for the sake of the writing as for the conveyance of information. The handwriting was exquisite, the kind girls with calligraphy kits fantasize about; writing was something to which he paid attention.

"My friend Josh," Susie said.

"This is the best letter I've ever read. Can I have his address?"

And so I wrote Josh back. ("I read the letter you wrote to Susie, and I just have to say, I've never read such a . . .") We began a correspondence that continued through the following school year, peaking at the moment we thought we might actually go to the same college and falling off the way high school friends do when he decided on another school instead. But throughout that summer and our senior year, he wrote to me from his suburb of Cincinnati and I wrote back from my suburb of New York.

Once in college, I forgot about Josh. But years later, back in New York, I was rifling through a copy of the *Washington Monthly* and saw his name on the masthead. I sent off a letter immediately. "I *knew* you were a good writer!" I exclaimed. We corresponded briefly and several years after that I found his name among the instructors teaching writing at the New School. I decided to surprise him by stopping by the first class to introduce myself.

"We meet at last!" I cried when he walked in. It had been nine years since our first letter exchange. Since then, we've e-mailed.

After the monthlong confinement in Mauriac, I was shipped out to my homestay with a commuter family in a nondescript suburb of Albi, birthplace of Henri de Toulouse-Lautrec, who had hightailed it to Paris, and one hour north of Toulouse, home of the French airline industry. The father was an engineer; the mother held a nondescript part-time office job and was Italian by birth. At first, I felt ripped off anew, as if her national origin made my French homestay somehow inauthentic. Wasn't I supposed to be learning about *French* culture? But she grew vegetables in the backyard and made a tomato tart that rivaled the best New York pizza. For the first time in my life, I ate tomatoes that weren't pinkish simulacrums from Burger King, biting into them like apples. I had nothing in common with this family but I grew to appreciate them.

The twin five-year-old girls were still learning to pronounce their French *r*'s, and I liked listening as they gurgled "*Encore! Encore!*" when they wanted another helping at dinner. I realized for the first time that when concert audiences cheer for an encore, they are actually pleading, "More! More!" like small children. The twins beat me handily at French Scrabble, which is pro-

nounced in French exactly how you think it would be pronounced. These losses stung, conveying to me in no uncertain
terms: You know nothing of this language. I still had so much to
learn.

But that was pretty much it as far as cultural immersion went.
With nowhere to go and no way to get there, I loitered around
the house like a sullen French teen, perusing La Redoute catalogs
and trying to make use of the Minitel, a pre-Internet networked
service that looked like a portable Apple II Plus. On the televi-
sion, I watched outdated episodes of the soap opera *Santa Barbara*,
in which a very young Robin Wright emoted in dubbed French. On
the radio, the pouty pop princess Vanessa Paradis had a hit song,
"Marilyn et John," which competed in heavy rotation against her
previous hit, "Joe Le Taxi." She would go on to star in a Chanel
commercial and have children with Johnny Depp; that summer
she breathily provided my life soundtrack.

Given that I was spending the summer lolling about, only
Frenchly, I was relieved to have brought my own books—Kurt
Vonnegut's *Slaughterhouse-Five*, Walter Lord's *A Night to Remember*. But once those were done, in an effort to absorb the language, I picked up a couple of native paperbacks from a rotating
rack at the local drugstore. Unfamiliar with contemporary Fran-
cophone literature and daunted by the prospect of Hugo or Balzac,
I went straight for the lesser challenge of American translation:
Daniel Keyes's *Flowers for Algernon* and Stephen King's *Salem's
Lot*, in *livre de poche* form for French escapists. Though I'd
already read both in English, I made it only several chapters into
each, winded by the effort.

Guiltily, I put an "inc." in the Book of Books next to these
lapses, an impromptu notation for "incomplete." Those "inc."s

bummed me out. A doer of assignments and a fan of last pages, I liked to finish what I began. Later in Bob, the "inc." became a more succinct empty square next to the title, noting in a more muted fashion when I gave up on a book. What I hated or couldn't finish or failed to grasp was often as telling as what I did manage to complete. Just like a regular diary, Bob would record my failings, however noble.

There was quite a bit of failure in store that summer. I didn't entirely learn to read in French and I didn't see the France I'd come to see and I didn't fully integrate into the culture or even bond with my fellow Americans abroad. The person I'd gotten to know best in France was spending his summer outside Cincinnati. Things were being left undone.

So it was only appropriate in the Book of Books with *The Trial*, a novel that never ends. This was not a perversely inspired stroke. When I'd picked it up, dazzled by Mikhail Baryshnikov's recent Broadway turn in *Metamorphosis*, I'd no idea Kafka never finished it. On the contrary, I'd urgently awaited the story's resolution, needed it—the meting out of punishment and forgiveness, the tying up of loose ends and righting of wrongs.

Instead, Joseph K. spends this last chapter refusing to kill himself, whereupon he is perfunctorily knifed to death in a brief final chapter. After this "ending," my edition moved on to several pages of unfinished chapters, deleted passages, diary excerpts, and assorted postscripts. Even with this bonus material, we never find out Joseph K.'s crime. Had Kafka intended to leave the crime unspecified, if there even was one? There was no way of knowing and no fellow Kafka readers to ask; there was no Internet to consult.

But finished or not, *The Trial* was the book I needed at the time, an apt metaphor for the extended bout of umbrage and frustration of adolescence. It is the teenager's lot to feel simultaneously innocent and guilty, accountable to grown-up society but not allowed in, bristling with potential yet largely powerless. How could you not be drawn to a book about a person falsely accused, harassed, and made to carry out a series of tasks he didn't want to do? I got out of *The Trial* exactly what I needed: Vindication. An excuse. An escape. A convenient metaphor. A hero with whom I could identify.

The Trial also made clear to me, in a way a book could but another person could not, where bitterness crossed into brattiness. Joseph K. was the subject of a gross injustice and heartless bureaucratic dudgeon; I'd merely accompanied him along the way, then broke for croissants.

But this was my own business. I marked the book down, in secret, in my new clandestine diary. I may have felt misunderstood and terrible at French, but you wouldn't be able to tell any of that from reading the pages of my personal journal, my most excellent yet still thoroughly true-to-me Bob. In this Book of Books, I'd be able to take charge of my own story and make it better.

CHAPTER 4

Catch-22

Never Enough

Some people are perfectly content with the mere reading of books. They take them out of the library, they borrow them from friends, they give them away with little expectation or even desire to see them returned. They download them onto devices where they exist in some ephemeral electronic format, never to be carefully stowed in a specific slot on a physical bookshelf or left to beckon from a nightstand or artfully piled on top of a coffee table. For these people, it's all about content. I envy their focus and their discipline.

Because there is also the other sort, the kind who gets all caught up in the rest of the book—even when it's not read. My sort wants the book in its entirety. We need to touch it, to examine the weight of its paper and the way text is laid out on the page.

People like me open books and inhale the binding, favoring the scents of certain glues over others, breathing them in like incense even as the chemicals poison our brains. We consume them.

We in this latter group like to own books, and, with our constant demands and high expectations, we're the worst—preferring some editions over others, having firm points of view on printings and cover designs. We're particular, and we're greedy. We want an unreasonable number of books and we don't like to throw them away. Some of us develop an almost hoardish fear around letting go of a book, even after it's been read and reread. Throwing away or lending a book to an unreliable reader inevitably leads to regret. It is lovely to share books, but they need to come home. I have known people to maintain years-long grudges over unreturned books. Who can blame them? (You with my Daniel Kahneman. You know who you are.)

Obviously, I want the books that I intend to read, but I also want the ones that I don't intend to read but think someone else I know might. Some books I may want to check back in on occasionally and I worry when they can't be found. Some books I need to have around "just in case." Just in case my daughter has to do a school project on French colonialism. Just in case one of my sons finally shows an interest in dinosaurs. Just in case one day I go to Ireland and need to consult the Irish classics. Or decide it's time to read *Gilgamesh*, or need a last-minute emergency gift.

I remember the moment my parents gave me my very first book, a soft fabric treasure called *The Pocket Book* that contained real, workable pockets you could open and close with a snap or a button. I could hardly believe such a spectacular creation existed and that it was mine. I wanted to climb inside *The Pocket Book* and snap it shut.

Part of me never fully left that welcoming interior or abandoned that giddy joy of ownership. I wanted to own more such things, a desire that remains unabated, even in my current state of plenty. If I pass a bookstore, I want to go in. When I see an especially sweet local library, my heart swells. Used bookstores contain untold possibilities. Library sales, same thing. There is always room for more books, even though I've barely dented the piles I already have.

Like all collectors, I exist in a perpetual state of want that bears no reasonable relationship to the quantity of unread books mountaining up on my shelves. Places to stack them are covered as soon as they surface; I keep adding new built-in bookshelves. At this point, there is no human way that I could read even those books I've deliberately marked as absolute must-reads. I own many times more books than are noted in my Book of Books, yet still I worry over his empty pages. I use a minuscule type when writing in my Book of Books in order to leave room for everything that needs to go there. Bob's pages, I used to fear, would one day run out. Now I fear I will die before I can fill them up.

This is every reader's catch-22: the more you read, the more you realize you haven't read; the more you yearn to read more, the more you understand that you have, in fact, read nothing. There is no way to finish, and perhaps that shouldn't be the goal. The novelist Umberto Eco famously kept what the writer Nassim Taleb called an "anti-library," a vast collection of books he had not read, believing that one's personal trove should contain as much of what you don't know as possible.

Some of my particular strain of want is certainly due to early deprivation. Books were—and still are—expensive, and my mother almost never purchased them. To this day, she waits for a title to become available while her name climbs up the library wait list. I remember picture books of my childhood like *The Pocket Book* so well precisely because there weren't many of them. We had *Richard Scarry's Busy, Busy Town* and his superb *I Am a Bunny* (a book that forever raised my sensory expectations for the changing seasons), the high-drama *Miss Suzy*, the unfathomable bounty of *Blueberries for Sal*. Especially in the recession seventies, decades before printing became inexpensive in China, hardcover picture books were practically a luxury product. The few we owned were shared among my brothers and me. I read more books about trucks than did most girls.

In my childhood bedroom, I had one meager bookshelf whose lower rung primarily accommodated back issues of *Young Miss* and *Seventeen*. With my ten-cent second grader's allowance, ratcheted up over the years into a weekly allotment never to exceed five dollars, I didn't have much money for books. Sometimes, I could afford comics or massive newsprint-quality compendiums sold at the dollar store with titles like *1,001 Wacky Facts*. Birthday checks were requisitioned for "college." If I asked my mother for a book, her standard response was "Get it from the library."

There wasn't much you could say back to that. Our house, a creaking hulk built in 1673, had actually been our town's first library; it had long since ceased to serve in that capacity, but we were just around the corner from the existing library, which was directly across from Main Street School. After dismissal, I'd cross the street and install myself for an hour or two.

While the library was, of course, a public institution, it felt private to me. The children's library shelves were mine. I knew where my friends Ginny and Geneva awaited and where the slightly naughtier Klickitat gang hung out at the end of the front row. The mean kids from *Deenie* and *Blubber* looked down from the high shelf. These characters provided my social life and I never had to be told to be quiet in their presence.

I wanted to crawl into the stacks and absorb the musty smell of decades-old paper. I riffled my fingers through the wooden card-catalog drawers like they were flip books, trying to decode them. I could be the first girl to master the Dewey decimal system. I might one day know where every book stood. All I needed was some authority or at least some kind of officially sanctioned status. A few years after we'd moved to town, I mustered the courage to ask for a job.

"I'm sorry, there are no jobs available for children," the librarian told me. I was ten.

"You wouldn't have to pay me," I insisted, my eyes gleaming with what surely came across as unhealthy fervor.

"That's okay, but thank you."

The rejection was terrible. What was it that put the children's librarian off my candidacy? Was it the you-don't-have-to-pay-me part? Did she question my intentions? Did she not see that I was a book person, different from other, more casual library visitors, that I cared? That I would never leave a book facedown with its spine splayed open like other kids my age. I couldn't help but feel they were taking me down a notch. "This library isn't *yours*, you know," is how I heard it.

Every once in a while, I'd gin up the pluck to inquire again, thinking maybe they wouldn't remember me from the last time. Sometimes asking at the children's library, other times going to the person at checkout with the enviable task of scanning each book through the ghostly red glow of the primitive computer system. These requests were always swiftly rebuffed, and each time I felt sorry for having had the temerity to ask. Perhaps they knew I was reading beyond my jurisdiction; someone in charge must have seen me with the Sweet Dreams.

Because the library limited the number of books you could check out at a time, I developed fantasies about coming into a large quantity of books. Our house had a basement whose walls crumbled at the touch. (Murderers lurked in the dark spaces behind staircases, and after seeing *Friday the 13th* at far too young an age I knew they were waiting to reach through and grab my ankles.) But there were untended boxes down there, too, and they might be filled with books if only I dared look. The other probable stash was in the allegedly inaccessible attic, a place we never once entered during our fourteen years in that house. Stowed away up there, I believed, was an immense trove of *Archie* comics and other goodies, perpetually kept out of reach.

Books in the living room were for grown-ups and not to be touched. My mother had a few coffee table books, which she guarded fiercely. I was allowed to read *Miss Piggy's Guide to Life* only under supervision, turning its pages gingerly and never removing it from the coffee table. My aunt had given it to my mother as a gift, and it was made clear that, despite appearances, *Miss Piggy's Guide to Life* was not a children's book.

My older brother Roger's books were not exactly children's books either; his were the literature of defiant male adolescence. What he liked to do was read *Jaws* when my mother forbade him from seeing the movie. Of all my family members, Roger was most like me; we even looked alike, though, as he liked to point out, my face managed to be both too long and too fat at the same time; his was merely too long. Roger and I shared the same twisted sense of humor that made other people frown when we laughed. My chief ambition was to get him to laugh against his will, sometimes achieved by adopting my signature Glazed Look during a staring contest or performing a spirited jig so foolish that merely glimpsing it as a passive observer proved embarrassing. Neither of us was socially successful. For his part, Roger blamed the chess club. "Thus sealing my social fate forever," he said.

According to some tacit regulation, Roger controlled the bathroom reading. Its inventory remained stable for years: *The Twilight Zone Companion*, an episode-by-episode guide complete with creepy stills ("Eye of the Beholder" in particular provided the stuff of nightmares); Stephen King's *Christine*, riveting despite being about a car; *The Fiske Guide to Colleges*, which gave me early and strong opinions about the undesirability of Swarthmore (all those nonliterary requirements!); *Uncle John's Bathroom Reader*, never as rewarding as its title suggested. I read them all, cover to cover, over and over.

None of it was enough.

Whenever my bank account managed to reach the double digits, I'd bring my blue passbook to the local branch and bike up to the used bookstore off Main Street to buy Nancy Drews. These purchases were carefully considered. "Do you have any new Nancy Drews?" I'd ask when I walked in, by which I meant old Nancy Drews, but not too old. I wanted nothing to do with the reissued paperbacks and their loathsome "contemporary" illustrations; the really ancient ones with their dark woven blue covers were also unacceptable.

But oh . . . the yellow-bound Nancy Drews, with their broody cover paintings and pen-and-ink interior images of the girl detective and friends, pixie-haired George and "plump" Bess. They sold for about a dollar a copy, an incredible bargain. Nancy Drew taught me that a book wasn't merely about the words within, it was everything—the quality of paper, the intoxicating smell of the binding glue, an older formulation that you didn't get in newer volumes, the decorative end pages. It was the book as object, the vase as much a pleasure as the flowers.

If the shopkeeper had no yellow Nancy Drews, I'd depart in haste, shrouded in remorse for having wasted his time. The poor guy with his forlorn shop that nobody ever went into. He probably lived for those precious moments when the bells jangled on the front door, dreaming of customers less particular about their mysteries. He probably scraped by on lunches of peanut butter and jelly and cursed the chain bookstore at the nearby mall. I constructed an entire narrative around the shopkeeper and my sorry role in his professional travails. Only after I'd graduated from high school and left town did I mention to my best friend, Ericka, how I'd suffered on his behalf.

"The used bookstore owner?" she replied, incredulous. "He was a millionaire! He just kept that shop for fun." Ericka knew all kinds of town stuff because her parents were entrenched in the community whereas my mom was strictly the commuter type.

I had one other book-buying opportunity and I shamelessly abused it. On Divorced Dad Thursdays, after I'd finished my strawberry French toast and strawberry milk shake and strawberry cheesecake at the diner, my father would often let my brothers and me run amok in the Barnes & Noble at the Roosevelt Field mall. My father was a construction contractor—"small jobs, Pammy"—and didn't have a lot of money to spare. He would warn on arrival that I could pick two or three books and no more, which he paid for with folded bills or hastily shuffled credit cards. I would nod, almost intending obedience, and then set out. An hour later I'd show up at the cash register with a tower of books wedged determinedly under my chin.

There was no helping it. Series like Choose Your Own Adventure were *meant* to be consumed whole, and the library must not have considered them worthy for its collection. Sidney Sheldon, Danielle Steel, both erratic presences at the library, beckoned in long, gleaming rows, breathless plots teased enticingly on their covers, brand-new, sometimes with embossed letters. I was really, really sorry but it was impossible to narrow things down.

"I don't want to have to say no to you when it comes to buying books," my dad would say, as I lobbied for please just one more. "If I'm going to spend money, then it should be on this." It was the best thing he could have said. I never forgot it and I never stopped feeling guilt ridden about taking it so literally.

But it still wasn't enough. Frustrated by my failure to gain employment at the library, I threw myself into the project of making money, not to buy clothes or makeup or records, but because I wanted not to have to depend on others—not in life, not in stories, not for books.

This wasn't always easy. When I was twelve, I started baby-sitting, but while my friends got to babysit toddlers who were already asleep in houses with poorly cataloged liquor cabinets, my wards were bad sleepers whose health-food-nut parents came home early and paid $3.35 an hour, precisely minimum wage, and never rounded up, rummaging through their pockets for the appropriate coins. In eighth grade, I was fired from my first "real job" at a real estate office for subpar typing, a stunning blow to my already tenuous self-conception. I couldn't type!

I envisioned a fantasy job that involved free food and ample downtime to read as I waited for the occasional customer. Instead, I stood on my feet all day at Butterfour Bakery, where roaches discouraged us from snarfing up the sprinkles. At a friend's mother's South American–import warehouse, I glued together catalogs in an empty room that reeked inexplicably of molasses. I folded sweaters at Laura Ashley in a store dense with the scent of Laura Ashley No. 1, prim women in headbands narrowing their eyes at my sloppy sleevework.

Throughout junior high and until I was seventeen, I slaved away three to five nights a week at a local restaurant. The married owner would alternate between muttering under his breath as he trailed his fingers over the small of my back: "I can't stand it— you're driving me mad with desire!" and yelling at me in front of the line cooks: "Don't lean on those counters, clean those counters!" As a reprieve, I worked at the Grand Union supermarket, where I dreamed up stories for each customer based on the items in front of me. ("She promised him he'd have meat loaf that night, if only he'd . . ." "He came in to get onions, but in aisle four he decided . . .") I liked to juggle several jobs at a time to alleviate the tedium of each post, five or six days a week after school, saving up.

Senior year, I arranged my schedule so that my classes ended at one o'clock. Skipping lunch meant I could rush off to whatever store or restaurant job was on my schedule that day. There was little time for extracurricular activities; Ericka and I founded the school's Coalition for the Poor and Homeless, but our efforts sputtered out after a few protests and one visit to a nearby soup kitchen. I felt increasingly untethered from the social world of high school, biding my time until I was free.

Finally, armed with a driver's license, I was able to find the kind of work I sought. Twenty minutes from my house, at the upscale Americana shopping center, was a branch of the B. Dalton bookstore chain—and they hired me.

Now *this* was a job! I was the only high schooler who worked there, a monumental achievement and a source of fierce pride, even if you considered there wasn't much competition. All the other employees were actual grown-ups, some of whom saw the job as a calling, others who could just as easily have been working in the produce section at the A&P.

Dan, the manager, was one of the former, a short, sweaty man in his midthirties with sparse tendrils of black hair clinging hopefully to his pate, and a mind brimming with knowledge acquired the hard way. He greeted my enthusiasm and ignorance with tolerant dismissiveness. He had informed opinions.

But I was determined to learn. I would know exactly what to read and what I would read next. My Book of Books would reflect this clear path forward. Here, at B. Dalton, I could keep my pulse on the passions of the nation; I just had to pay attention. I quickly noticed, for example, that whenever a book broke out in a big way, someone from management ordered rising swirls of that title that spiraled up majestically from the floor. Only senior employees knew how to build and maintain these symmetrical assemblages. Regular sales clerks like me were not allowed to touch them.

Massive cardboard displays—known in the trade as "dumps"—loomed over the aisles, where they signaled the defining cultural events of the day. Over here, pillars of *Bonfire of the Vanities.* Over there, an imposing tower of Stephen Hawking's *A Brief History of Time*, which everyone in the we're-sophisticated suburbs just had to have. I would caress this slender volume longingly, imagining that if I owned it, my true place in the universe would make itself known. I envied the people who could just stroll in and purchase a few hardcovers off the important towers with the swipe of a credit card.

Somewhere along the main aisle stood a commanding dump of *Dianetics*. These must be important, I mused, leafing through a copy during an idle moment.

"What do you think you're doing?" Dan barked.

"Just curious," I said guardedly. "What is this?"

"You don't want to know," he muttered with a quick wave of his hand. I put down the L. Ron Hubbard in a state of unquenched curiosity, too nervous to get caught going near it again. There were so many mysteries that eluded my beginner's grasp of the world of letters.

"What's this?" I inquired, holding up one of Joseph Campbell's books on mythology. Who *was* Joseph Campbell and why was he so important?

"What's this?" I asked, pointing to a swirl of *Clan of the Cave Bear* with the mermaid from *Splash* inexplicably crawling across its cover. How did *this* book get to be a movie and what did that mean? So many books indicated something significant yet inscrutable. Authors seemed to have reputations I couldn't quite deconstruct. Stuart Woods dominated an entire shelf—a monolith of contemporary letters? Ann Rule, master of criminal justice?

Then, the threat of crime itself came to B. Dalton. In 1989, when Ayatollah Khomeini in Iran issued a fatwa against Salman Rushdie for his novel *The Satanic Verses*, my colleagues and I were swept up into what felt like a mission of global import. The only time I'd given thought to Iran prior to this was during the hostage crisis, when someone graffitied "Fuck the Ayatollah" on a building near Main Street School, where it remained for the rest of my grade-school education. Every time I looked at it, I thought, "The world is full of mysterious danger."

But this current danger was exciting. I became nearly delirious in my desire to sell *The Satanic Verses*, spellbound by photographs of Rushdie's daunting eyebrows and pungent gaze. The tapping of cash register buttons was swiftly upgraded into a campaign to save literature from the forces of darkness. I blazed with excitement.

Each day my coworkers and I reported for duty to get the latest instructions, direct from corporate headquarters. Copies of Rushdie's book were to be kept near the cash registers. No, *behind* the cash registers. No, now in the back of the store, the stockroom, where only management could tread. Employees who did not feel safe selling the book were allowed to be taken off the schedule, no repercussions. People were bombing bookstores!

Suburban customers who couldn't for their lives tell the difference between Iran and Iraq (I counted myself among them) flocked in droves to our store, whether out of curiosity, for political purposes, or simply to feel part of something. They skulked up to the cash register, saying—in the hushed tones of a John le Carré character—they wanted to buy The Book. "If somebody asks whether we stock it or not, think carefully before you reply," we were told. "Answer on a case-by-case basis."

"What's the book about?" I asked Dan.

"Nobody knows," he replied.

In any case, it was a hardcover. Nonmanagerial employees received a 5 percent discount on merchandise, the barest acknowledgment of our contributions. The closest B. Dalton came to giving workers a free book was during inventory. On these evenings, the store stayed open late and in the cloak of darkness stripped those mass-market paperbacks deemed unsellable and shipped them off to be pulped. Under Dan's supervision, we tore their covers off, lobbing the denuded copies into a dumpster.

The whole thing was upsetting. Books were sacred objects, something I wouldn't dream of throwing away. Well trained by the library, I considered the idea of defacing a book, even with thoughtful marginalia, a punishable offense. I couldn't believe an item of such import could just be torn apart, its carefully designed cover ripped ruthlessly from its guts, and jettisoned to a place where no one would read it.

We weren't supposed to take these rejects, though Dan uncharacteristically gave me a pass. The trouble was, shorn of their casings, whatever allure these books may have once held—and there was little; they were, after all, trashed for a reason—was lost in their newly abused state. I felt sullied in the process, as ripped off as the books themselves.

My B. Dalton career, in the end, only whetted my appetite. What were all those books about, why were people buying them, and when could I?

Meanwhile, upstate where he and my stepmother escaped the confines of their middle-income housing complex, my father had developed a library-sale habit, scooping up reams of former bestsellers for pennies. These books, though used, somehow felt found rather than lost. He gathered old James Micheners, well-worn histories of the Catskills, any book about the Spanish Civil War, photographic collections of military hardware, and what felt like more than enough copies of John Dos Passos's *U.S.A.* trilogy. He had a weakness, which I contracted through osmosis, for books that had enjoyed a moment of wild popularity decades earlier and then managed to fade into obscurity. (My brother

Roger inherited this same tendency, assembling a Library of the Absurd in his living room, which included such treasures as the complete oeuvre of Phyllis Schlafly.)

I combed my dad's newly stocked shelves and there, nestled between Ulster County histories and books about the Lincoln Brigade, I came across a used mass-market paperback of Joseph Heller's *Catch-22*, a book that struck me as an especially sophisticated choice for a high schooler. It was not a classic in the English-class sense of the word nor was it a children's book. It was just a book grown-ups read. I wanted to partake in that, not for edification but for fun.

Catch-22 was a book about war and geopolitics—about which I knew precisely nothing. But more than its unfamiliar subject matter, its distinctive associative style, its circular structure, its repetitive and escalating iterations were completely unlike the straightforward narratives I'd trained on. Perhaps even more important, *Catch-22* was the first book that made me laugh out loud (apart from giggling over picture books). Hungry Joe, who dreamt every night he had a cat sleeping on his face and finally woke to find he had a cat sleeping on his face, made me spit out my food.

When I wasn't upstate, I worked weekends in the city. I'd read on the Long Island Rail Road to Penn Station, stop briefly at one of "my" Barnes & Nobles, on the corner of Thirty-Fourth and Seventh, then take the subway uptown to Madison Avenue. There I worked at a small French clothing store, selling one-size-fits-all viscose dresses in loud patterns, mostly to keep up my language skills. I chatted with my French colleagues during the largely empty hours and, an incorrigible mimic, wound up speaking English in a haughty French accent whenever a customer walked in, a habit that endeared me to exactly no one.

I worked so hard at all of these jobs, not because I loved them but because they were a means to an end, one that had nothing to do with the jobs themselves or adding value to my college application. What I wanted was resources and freedom, the means to buy books and to know which books to buy.

The core of *Catch-22* is, of course, its titular phrase, one used to describe an unsolvable logical dilemma that keeps people in their place, typically a lowly one. This idea entered the popular vernacular and took hold with such ubiquity that it's hard to understand how we ever got by without it. My personal catch-22 was the unquenchable yearning to own books—to own books and to suck out the marrow of them and then to feel sated rather than hungrier still. I couldn't have been more deluded.

CHAPTER 5

The Norton Anthology
of English Literature

Required Reading

Denounce the canon all you want; it's hard to shake the conviction that certain books are meant to be read. Books you may have to struggle to finish. Books that everyone else seems to have read and anyone who dares consider himself a reader, or at the very least "well read," will also have read, whether they enjoy the experience or not. It's why everyone gets defensive when you bring up the subject of James Joyce's *Ulysses*. People still feel that to be a real reader, you have to . . . someday. (For the record: I haven't.)

As a child, I assumed one of these books was the encyclopedia. In its entirety. It was just a matter of hunkering down, and I actually thought I could do it. If only we'd owned the *World Book*. Instead we were cursed with a yellowed edition of the *Encyclopaedia Britannica*, passed down from some forgotten relative, its infrequent and uninspired black-and-white line drawings a pale comparison to the enviable full-color splendor of the *World Book*. Time and again I would set myself to read one of its mouse-brown volumes, almost hairy with age, and find my mind traipsing off elsewhere within paragraphs.

The canon also included, in my youthful estimation, any book with "classic" on its cover, a word imbued with near-magical powers, no matter how abridged and watered down the rendition. (A series of "chunky" classic books, adorable in their four-by-three-inch format, with pen-and-ink illustrations and sold on a stationery-store spinning rack, led me to believe I had polished off *The Three Musketeers* and *The Hunchback of Notre Dame*.) The canon included anything by a Great Writer, someone famous enough to be an occasional character in a movie or TV show or another book. It included anything associated with Western civilization, the only civilization I'd learned about from school.

Part of this imperative stemmed from insecurity. If you're going to be a bookish child, you had damn well better be good at it, and I feared the prospect of being sniffed out for my lapses. Someone always has to be the person who has never read Trollope, but it damn sure wasn't going to be me. When a book wasn't assigned at school, I assigned it to myself.

In my Book of Books, I appended an asterisk to those Famous Books I'd personally selected: *Madame Bovary, The 42nd Parallel, The American Political Tradition*. Unlike my earlier teenage childhood diaries, which made me squirm when I looked through them, Bob's entries, I determined, would make me proud.

Even as a preschooler, I instinctively believed that certain picture books were better than others; they had silver and gold embossed medals on their covers or had managed to survive alongside boldly colored stories despite black-and-white engraved illustrations. I could sniff out books that were clearly unworthy like a bedbug dog. Bad books were cheap and poorly produced; they had garish illustrations or dumbed-down text; they were about visits to the dentist or stupid-looking bears trying to get along. Who thought this was okay for young people? If you're trying to lift a child up, the last thing you should do is talk down to her. I took this underestimation personally.

This is how you get primed from an early age to worship at the canon's imposing altar. In high school, I enrolled in AP English, where we read only Great Books: Faulkner and Joyce and Conrad and Fitzgerald. Our teacher was a believer in modernism and close textual reading. I was not. Where were all the proper nouns? I struggled to keep my eyes on the page and not on my teacher's nose, which, with its spiky mesh of hair protruding from each nostril, drew me in like a beacon. At any moment, he might demand we locate a specific phrase from Faulkner's *Go Down, Moses*, and even insist that we understand it. I could ill afford to get lost in the tangle. He was especially fond of quizzing us on the first three pages of *A Portrait of the Artist as a Young Man*. I lived in fear of not knowing something about the moocow.

It never once occurred to me to skip my assigned reading, no matter how unappealing. I even went one maddening step further: I read it early. I read everything as soon as it was assigned, did all my homework, wrote my essay, and handed it in. This drove friends and roommates crazy, but what they didn't understand was that I was driven by fear, and also, perversely, by a form of laziness and impatience. I really wanted to just get it over with now and move on to the next item. There were lots of books needing to be read.

I remember the precise moment in grade school when I bailed on procrastination, which up until then had been my standard modus operandi, as it is for most daydreamy children. I was pushing a pencil through the grayish-pink carpet of my bedroom, avoiding one task or another, when I had an epiphany: If something needed to get done, I could put it off and worry about it and then do the actual task. Or I could just do it right away and then go back to pushing pencils through the carpet. I chose the latter, because it meant that in the aggregate you had less to do. Also, you had less chance of getting in trouble for not getting something done. Cowed by authority, I went about life convinced that, at any moment, someone would give me a good, hard look that said, "You there. Yes, you. Did you *really* do what you were supposed to do?" I was not going to get caught.

Conquering *The Norton Anthology of English Literature* felt fundamental to this plan. The most required of all requirements, the *Norton Anthology* is the bedrock of every college English literature survey, and the foundational text for any English major. By college graduation, anyone who considered himself remotely literary was supposed to have a well-worn duct-taped copy on his shelf.

"The *Norton Anthology* was based on the idea that it actually matters to plunge into a comic masterpiece written in the 1300s or to weep at a tragedy performed in the 1700s," Stephen Greenblatt, one of its editors, has explained. "It is vitally important to remind people that the humanities carry the experience, the lifeforms of those who came before us, into the present and into the future. Through reading literature we can make ghosts speak to us, and we can speak back to them."

I wasn't the only person to bow before the *Norton*'s demands.

"It turns out many students—without the compulsion of their teachers—feel that they really shouldn't go through their undergraduate years without reading the great imaginative works of the past," Greenblatt said. This describes precisely how I felt in the fall of 1989, my first semester in college, a budding English major. If I was worth anything as a reader, I was going to read that *Norton*—if not quite cover to cover, then at least enough to constitute a thorough sampling of the essentials, no matter how mind-numbing.

So eager was I that I preenrolled in the English Department's yearlong survey of English literature, where the *Norton* ruled supreme. I would soon know "the basics," once and for all. At the Brown bookstore I splurged on a brand-new copy, a brick of a book containing 2,616 paper-thin pages, which I intended to make bountiful use of so that every sign of wear signified an acquired bit of knowledge. My *Norton*, the first volume of the book's fifth edition, included Shakespeare and Swift and Johnson. It also contained Middle English lyrics like "Fowls in the Frith" and "My Lief Is Faren in Londe," along with the interminable "Sir Gawain and the Green Knight," part of the so-called Alliterative Revival, written in unfathomable Old English verse. ("The borgh brittened and brent to brondes and askes," etc.)

And it contained Edmund Spenser's *The Faerie Queene*, a nefarious bit of doggerel disguised beneath a deceptively enchanting title. Is there any more dispiriting way to enter the canon than *The Faerie Queene*? I couldn't make heads or tails of it. Years later, I took comfort in the unimpeachable literary critic Terry Castle's own recollection: "I still have my old paperback copy of Spenser's poem and just looking at it—the pages and pages of bewildering verse in tiny print, the demented little crib notes

I've scribbled in the margins—can induce in me a sort of mental seasickness . . . so dense with weird archaisms and arcane symbols, bizarre characters, confusing plots and subplots."

But I didn't know Castle's work at the time. When I looked around my English class, the other students appeared to be fully absorbed. It didn't occur to me in my greenness that they might all just be exceptionally persuasive fakers. I took it as an indictment of my ill-preparedness.

The Faerie Queene also made one suspected failure official: I would never understand poetry. It was one of my many deficiencies as a reader, but it was perhaps the most damning. Poetry was practically a litmus test for literary credibility. Real book lovers loved poetry, yet for me it remained opaque. When I encountered poetry in a collection, I couldn't help flipping the pages until the paragraphs reverted to the reassuring tempo of prose.

I'd started off, as most children do, with poetic promise. I adored nonsense verse, full of as much respect for Dr. Seuss and Shel Silverstein as the next second grader. In third grade, thinking I was possibly gifted when it came to verse, I wrote my first poem, a contemplative ode to the tree, which received a certain amount of praise from the teacher. It was at precisely this point that my ability to create and appreciate poetry stalled. I did have an idea for a follow-up effort, one about a road with two paths, which I shared with my mother. "I think that's taken," she said.

The Norton Anthology of English Literature was positively riddled with poetry, much of it in older forms of English that brought back eighth-grade memories of stumbling through *The Canterbury Tales*. I read the words dumbly, I reread them, I thought about what to eat for breakfast and about the StairMaster and about Joe, who with his rumpled rugby gear and prep-school face sat rapt during the entire discussion of *The Faerie Queene* and, what's more, participated, his palpable appreciation leaving me shorn of depth and cultivation. Even Joe the rugby player got it.

I understood that *The Faerie Queene* was meant to transport me, but I failed to take flight. I never even got off the ground, my mind darting furtively to Joe, who always slid nonchalantly into his chair just moments before class began looking like he'd tumbled directly out of a frat-house bunk bed. My crush on him was unbearable and unquestionably apparent to all others in the class who no doubt looked on me with pity. Maybe Joe, too, hoped to meet someone "serious" in English. But surely he had his eyes set on the kind of girl who liked poetry; girls who liked poetry were more alluring. My romances with him and with verse felt equally hopeless. (Years later, on a moonlit night in Istanbul, I walked along, silent and deflated, as my boyfriend at the time and my friend Mindy rapturously quoted Gerard Manley Hopkins from memory in an escalating back-and-forth. I had only two poems memorized: "Clouds" and "The Woodpecker," both by Shel Silverstein.)

Soon, and even worse, I encountered a class that completely defeated my pledge to finish assigned reading. All the other students in Martha Nussbaum's "Love and Literature" philosophy course sat at attention as the exalted philosopher expounded on her own impenetrable book and others equally opaque while I mentally took off for SeaWorld. I couldn't get through a single book she assigned, opening each one, slogging through two pages, and closing it, beaten. I couldn't even manage *To the Lighthouse*, earning the black mark for those failed women who somehow get through a liberal arts education without developing a reverence for Virginia Woolf.

College was full of lessons about just how much I didn't know. Despite what I'd learned growing up in a proud suburban school district, I quickly discovered that private education wasn't just for kids thrown into Catholic school as a form of punishment. Boarding school was not, in fact, a Dickensian prison sentence. Even my "good" suburban high school wasn't nearly as good as the "really good" suburban high schools—the ones in Brookline, Massachusetts, and Winnetka, Illinois. Lots of people knew a lot more than I did, and I was behind, no matter how diligently I completed my assignments.

I was haunted by the blackest scar on my record, one I never spoke of and rarely admitted to myself. When I'd moved to my new town back in second grade, I hadn't been placed in the highest reading group, but in the second highest. It was a setback so humiliating that I never told my parents, and when I was later moved up to the higher group, it was an achievement I could share with no one. Perhaps that second-grade teacher had known something about me, some inherent intellectual flaw that I would never shake, no matter how hard I tried.

Worst of all was the realization that mere effort wouldn't catch me up. I may have considered myself a "book person," but that didn't mean I was a good reader. My college classmates seemed to read better than I did, drawing meanings and making inferences I hardly noticed. They shared this greater understanding in seminars, speaking with an eloquence I could hardly muster. In English class, I grew progressively quieter, retreating into early-childhood shyness.

This failure to master the greats of the *Norton* robbed me of the literary confidence with which I'd swaggered into college. My B. Dalton mall experience reshelving Nelson Demilles paled in comparison with the learned discussions private school kids had enjoyed in their Western Civ seminars. Here, I was not even cut out for the basics. I wouldn't major in English after all. I wouldn't, in fact, take a single writing class in college. I rejected it preemptively, deciding to major in history instead.

While some people feel pressure to read the latest novel, my particular neurosis has always been to catch up on writers who died long ago yet endure still. Their words had achieved a kind of permanence; they mattered. That's why the *Norton* was so important, and so crushing in its judgment. Even when an authority figure didn't outwardly assign reading, my internal schoolmarm did the job, berating me for various deficiencies. Why haven't you read Trollope, I'd scold myself. If you're going to read Richard Ellmann's *Wilde*, you also have to read his *Joyce*. Read Greek plays.

This was the era of Allan Bloom's *The Closing of the American Mind*. Like most Americans, I didn't have a clue, and I took the blow personally. How to traverse the gaping crevasses of ignorance without risk of exposure, in a way that didn't involve Joe?

I'd just have to work the canon on my own; only Bob would know what was going on. That summer, I took it on myself to become the one person alive to read through *The Dictionary of Cultural Literacy*, a book clearly never meant to have been read cover to cover. E. D. Hirsch, I figured, would tell me "What Every American Needs to Know." I proceeded to fill Bob with fundamental text after fundamental text, trying to find out what it was that everyone else seemed to know already. To prove that the identity I'd staked out—reader, writer, student, serious person—still held. I marked all this remedial reading in my Book of Books, where no one else could see what I was doing.

Oh, the shame of being underread, incapable of keeping up with even my own demands, let alone the expectations for the Ivy League English major. I didn't realize until much later in life that nearly everyone, except those lucky bastards who can devote themselves 24-7 to the task, feels this way, too. It wasn't until I was in my thirties that I understood it was okay and even right to read what you wanted rather than what you ought.

But at college this did not feel like a smart state of mind. All around me, semiotics majors had an ambitious agenda, busily deconstructing every subject into smithereens. A surfeit of criticism swirled around campus, yet I still didn't understand what it was we were meant to critique. I still wanted to take in what they wanted to tear down. I wanted to believe, not disdain. I wanted to absorb, not fend off. I wasn't ready to have a critical opinion. To quote Virginia Woolf, "If we could banish all such preconceptions when we read, that would be an admirable beginning. Do not dictate to your author; try to become him. Be his fellow-worker and accomplice. If you hang back, and reserve and criticize at first, you are preventing yourself from getting the fullest possible value from what you read." Instead, Woolf urged, "open your mind as widely as possible . . . and it will bring you into the presence of a human being unlike any other." If only I'd read her at the time.

CHAPTER 6

Into That Darkness

Voyeurism

"I'm going to read *The Rise and Fall of the Third Reich*," I informed
my dad the summer after freshman year of college. Now I'd
done it. My ambitions had been made public and I couldn't lose
face. The book would have to be read.

For years, I'd stared up at William Shirer's doorstopper of a
history, looming from my father's war bookshelf among endless guides to military aircraft and illustrated weaponry, like a
dare. Someone had once suggested with probable sarcasm that if
I wanted to know anything when it came to World War II, I'd
have to read Shirer.

And so I would, and, I also knew, despite the dauntingly
thick spine, I would love it. Give me a dark premise—dying,
death, murder, genocide—I am there. This is more a confession

than a boast. Many people I knew, several in my own family, almost religiously avoid books and movies about the Holocaust. Why would you even want to go there, they wonder, as if learning about it made you complicit, a sick curiosity. (My father, however, could read endlessly about the war's killing machinery, to me equally baffling.) It wasn't the acts of violence that fascinated me; it was how they could happen, and what it meant once they did.

I don't think the desire to read about these things can be entirely reduced to prurience. Part of it, I tend to think, is the opposite, a kind of yearning not only for answers but also for comfort. Dark books say to us, "This isn't about you. *You* are in fact alive and safe." Yes, there's an implicit and unavoidable warning, an edge of danger; these things happen, the books say. And yet, as bad as it gets inside this book, you, the reader, are securely outside.

If I'd actually bothered to complete any of the reading for Martha Nussbaum's class, I might have come across her own writing about the purpose suffering in literature holds for readers. "When we have emotions of fear and pity toward the hero of a tragedy, we explore aspects of our own vulnerability in a safe and pleasing setting," Nussbaum observed. This not only allows us to access our own emotions, it also enables us to cultivate empathy for others. You can't truly know how something feels unless you experience it, but reading about those experiences gives you a semblance.

Like many other morbid kids with Jewish ancestry, I was drawn to Holocaust reading from the moment I entered adolescence, seeking out the death and torture and deprivation and evil. The high point (or low) may have been Gitta Sereny's *Into*

That Darkness: An Examination of Conscience, based on interviews with Franz Stangl, the former commandant of Treblinka, which I immediately followed up with Sereny's *The Case of Mary Bell: A Portrait of a Child Who Murdered*. Reading these books about how tenuous and scary life is, I feel, at a gut level, more alive and more keenly aware of the startling tenuousness of that existence.

My old friend from France, Franz Kafka, perhaps put it best, describing not just the draw but also the necessity of dark reading. "I think we ought to read only the kind of books that wound and stab us. If the book we're reading doesn't wake us up with a blow on the head, what are we reading it for?" he wrote to a childhood friend. "We need the books that affect us like a disaster, that grieve us deeply, like the death of someone we loved more than ourselves, like being banished into forests far from everyone, like a suicide. A book must be the axe for the frozen sea inside us."

Back and forth on the Long Island Rail Road to the city, where I was spending a summer working for my stepmother's promotional items company, *The Rise and Fall of the Third Reich* did more than just break through the tedium. I ran the gamut of human emotion every day on that train. I'd flinch and tear up and tremble as I turned the pages, if the skin on my body had been scrubbed and exfoliated raw—and yet somehow, at the same time, I felt more reassured each time the train pulled into the station, safe.

This was not my first foray into the Holocaust nor would it be my last, because I wanted to take it one step further. A year later, while on a semester abroad in France, I developed a penchant for a kind of literary tourism unavailable to me on Long Island. My mother came to visit me in Paris, where I was then studying, and offered to take me to a city of my choice for a mother-daughter vacation. "Anywhere you like!" she said with visions of Saint-Tropez.

"I want to go to Besançon," I told her. I not only wanted to see the provincial hell Julien Sorel had been so anxious to flee in Stendhal's *The Red and the Black*, I also was keen on visiting a small exhibit devoted to the artwork of concentration camp victims from inside the camps. The collection featured tiny decrepit figurines carved out of soap and drawings etched in human ash. My mother, not sharing my unholy fascination, did not appreciate our destination as much as I did.

Luckily, I shared this particular if troubled passion with another family member: my cousin Kirsten. If there was one person to whom I could pass along a book about Josef Mengele's twin experiments and not get a look of sickened dismay in return, it was Kirsten, the daughter of my mother's only sister. Though she lived across the country, she and I had more in common than I did with most of my brothers. Over time, the four-year age gap between us collapsed, and she went from being my little cousin to the sister I'd always yearned for.

I considered it my personal mission to rescue Kirsten from the crystal meth–strewn cultural wasteland of her Colorado Springs high school. That summer, I begged my aunt to allow Kirsten to join me on a six-week Eurail tour of Europe. "I think she needs it," I said obliquely. To our shock, she consented. I brought along the books and the deal was I'd pass each one afterward to Kirsten, who also was the only person on the planet—how I loved her for this!—who read everything I asked her to read. Not only that, she read it immediately and remarkably fast, polishing off in a day what took me a week. That very summer when she got home to Colorado, she started a Book of Books of her own; the growth of her tally was swift. (Years later, when I wrote about Bob in the *Times*, she e-mailed at once: "So *that's* where I got the idea!")

Kirsten alone understood that I had to make a brief stop at Berchtesgaden, Hitler's getaway in southern Germany, on my way to meet up with her in Vienna. But Berchtesgaden had been turned into a restaurant and tourist destination, dulling the anticipated impact. Luckily, Kirsten and I had further plans. In Vienna, we met at the airport, and after a week of eating strudel in Viennese cafés, the two of us embarked on a much-anticipated tour of anti-Semitic Europe, heading first to Budapest and then to the Hungarian hinterland; the more wretched the history the more eager we were to check it out. We gave each other nicknames, Krakow Kirsten and Potsdam Pam, and decided to spend the majority of the trip speaking in heavy Borscht Belt accents. We were excited to hit all the major former ghettos of Eastern Europe.

Kirsten had been to Dachau as a young child, when her father was stationed at an air force base in Germany, but her memories of the experience were sketchy. We plotted our trip carefully, taking two days' worth of trains to get from Eger, the second-largest city in Hungary, to our final destination: Auschwitz. We'd always wanted to go.

En route, we were awakened repeatedly, first by Hungarian border guards, then by Czechs, and finally by Poles, each demanding various documents and, maddeningly, a ticket supplement that we didn't have and couldn't possibly obtain at this stage. In an effort to divert attention from the missing ticket, Kirsten and

I took to photographing each official who entered our car. The officials, men in their early twenties with pasty Eastern European complexions, wrapped their arms around our shoulders as they blushingly posed for each shot, occasionally kissing our cheeks with shy enthusiasm. We made it to Krakow without paying the supplementary fare.

Upon arrival at Oświęcim, just outside Krakow, a throng of guides descended on us with signs meant to entice: "Come to Auschwitz! Lunch and Birkenau included. Good morning!" Freaked out to see our gruesome interest thrown back in our faces so crassly, we rushed past them and took a local train, walking through a small town and then a field to get to the former death camp, asking people along the way, "Can you tell us how to get to Auschwitz?" Posing the question aloud to strangers sounded terribly wrong. There was no good way to translate with hand gestures to the uncomprehending locals.

We had planned to spend the entire day at Auschwitz. I'd thought reading books prepared me for anything. But what I had experienced as a kind of literary rubbernecking, there-but-for-the-grace-of-God-go-I, read from the safety of the Long Island Rail Road, affected me in a profoundly different way when I actually encountered the cavernous furnaces of Auschwitz. Within moments, Kirsten and I lost our sense of humor and the ironic remove. We stopped making fun of the kitschy guides and the absence of food stalls and the unnerving fact that we had chosen to be there. We found ourselves silenced by the immense oven doors, the glass-walled rooms filled with forever-lost eyeglasses and decaying leather shoes. Without the protection of a book cover, we had no way to distance ourselves from the implications.

"Do you want to leave?" I asked Kirsten when we walked out of a chamber we'd realized was a room-size oven.

"Yes," she said immediately.

Afterward, subdued and haunted, we headed to Berlin. That summer, a street parade of disaffected youth was all the rage. Massive floats and loud music crashed their way down the main thoroughfare. Instead of celebratory punks and drunken teenagers, we saw neo-Nazis and just plain Nazis. It was as if Auschwitz had spilled out the contents of the books we'd read and forced us to examine how they fit into the real world. We checked in at a few art museums but avoided the one dedicated to the war. Then we took off for Denmark and spent a drunken night at Tivoli on the park's giant roller coaster, trying to shake it off. It would be ten years before I went back to Germany.

CHAPTER 7

The Grapes of Wrath

Among Readers

It's the spring of 1992, and I'm sitting at a massive dining room table piled with obscure meats and homemade pâté and torn baguettes and overflowing ashtrays and a bunch of French people. The children are sitting with the adults rather than shunted off to a kiddie table, the way it's done at home. Extremely French authors like Le Clézio and Patrick Modiano are the subjects of animated conversation. Teenagers are allowed to talk, and the adults listen to them. It is a revelation.

So there *were* people who talked about books and ideas at dinnertime, quoting and debating and rhapsodizing—and it turned out they were in Paris. There were parents who recommended books to their children and discussed them together afterward. Students who read even when their grades didn't depend on it. Teenagers who could assume their friends also read—for fun, and not just "fun" reading. After a childhood of dinners at which people fought over how much broccoli they had to eat, sat in dogged silence, or monologued through their day's schedule, I entered this new dining landscape at age twenty. Never mind that they were eating stewed bunny rabbits; I felt at home.

And though my French wasn't the best, I very much wanted to be a part of it. When the talk at the dinner table turned to Steinbeck, I decided to muster my way into the conversation. This was American literature, after all, and they had a bona fide American on hand. Everyone would be dying to hear what I had to say. Bursting with collegiate ardor, I waited for an appropriate lull before making my contribution.

"*Les prunes de la fureur!*" I broke out excitedly.

There was silence. A neat oval of blank French facial expressions gaped at me.

"*Les quois?*" someone finally asked.

"*Les prunes de la fureur?*" I repeated, a smidge less sure.

"*Les* quois *de la fureur?*" Slowly.

Really?! Could they not know? Was it possible *The Grapes of Wrath*, celebrated paean to the working classes, was not part of the Steinbeck oeuvre revered by the unrepentantly socialist French?

Well, sure, it was possible. The French did have their cultural blind spots, often about American things. They were occasionally odd in their choice of artistic icons, persuaded that becoming a Bond girl was an untarnished achievement for a French actress, for example. Come to think about it, the dinner gathering had only been talking about *Travels with Charley*, *Of Mice and Men*, and *Cannery Row*. Had I found a gap in their knowledge?

I had not. I had found a gap in my French.

"*Les raisins de la colère!*" someone suddenly shrieked into the silence with a flash of insight. "*Les raisins de la colère!*" everyone repeated, bursting into laughter. Of course everyone at the table knew *The Grapes of Wrath*.

What had I said? *The Plums of Fury.* I went purple with embarrassment, only slightly less severe for having committed the error in a foreign language. For weeks after the incident, people joyously repeated "*Les prunes de la fureur!*" whenever they saw me or caught me making a simple grammatical error.

But here's what made the mockery bearable: they all got the joke. There was no need to articulate why it was funny or describe the special humiliation that happens when you try to sound smart about a book and fail. These people were readers. Nobody thought you pretentious for bringing up a work of classic literature. I belonged here.

Up until now, reading had been a lonely pursuit. During the benighted eighties, kids didn't go to bookstore readings or await the next Harry Potter on bustling lines at midnight. There were no embossed buttons or fan clubs for favored series. Children didn't tweet at authors or enter a chat room to compare *Wings of Fire* dragon tribes with other followers.

Though not quite in the same damning category as chess, reading was far from lacrosse in the high school pecking order. No one ever discussed it. In college, books assigned for class were read as competitive sport—the more critically, the better—and no one seemed to have time to read for pleasure. You didn't talk about liking a book; you ripped it to pieces.

The Mathieus were the first family of dedicated readers I'd met. They passed cherished volumes insistently among themselves like household secrets. My new French "parents," Carole and Bertrand Mathieu—she oversaw a research department at the École Polytechnique, he was an architect—had just purchased their Paris apartment with a small inheritance so Carole could live part-time in the city and send her older daughter to a prestigious high school in the Marais, while Bertrand stayed at their house in Picardy. It was an unusual arrangement, even for the French. Carole thought it good for a married couple not to see each other so much. I thought she was brilliant.

Carole and Bertrand were die-hard *soixante-huitards*, committed socialists, and thorough French traditionalists, with strong opinions. Architecture, according to Bertrand, was life's highest calling. He had little stickers inciting you to "Dare to be an architect" stuck to various surfaces around the house. Carole loved working at her office, even though she couldn't care less about business management, the section she oversaw. She smoked two packs of filterless Gitanes a day and held anyone who didn't smoke in contempt; people who had an occasional cigarette were similarly worthless. She refused to drink water, which she found repugnant, but always had a glass of whiskey at cocktail hour *"comme un bon alcolo."* Once a year, she took a solo vacation at the cottage Bertrand had built for them on an island in Brittany. "I stare at the ocean and read my books, all by myself. *C'est mer-veill-eux.*"

My sixteen-year-old "little sister," Juliette, would finish her schoolwork and then smoke in her bedroom over Dostoyevsky at night. Years later, after getting a doctorate in biogenetics and while working at the Institut Pasteur, she would read all of Zola's novels to get through her first pregnancy. Just like all American women do.

Books lined the walls of their apartment and the shelves of

their ramshackle country house. Bathrooms teemed with BDs (*bandes dessinées*, or graphic novels, a form the French were considerably more advanced in) and paperback fiction in translation from Tunisia, sub-Saharan Africa, Poland, and the American West. At night, the Mathieus dispersed, paperbacks in tow. "I am *with* my book now, *in* my bed," was a common refrain. My bedroom on the rue Rambuteau was a tiny nook of a room where, nestled like a kid in a tent, I, too, would read for hours. Of course, I told the Mathieus all about my Book of Books, and of course, they got Bob right away. "*Quelle bonne idée!*" Carole declared.

In France, the stakes in literature class were comfortably low; nobody in the study-abroad program was actually there to study. But the structure of the course allowed us to fake it, literally. Each week, we were given a reading assignment in French and then asked to write a "pastiche" in that particular writer's style. We read Proust's "La prisonnière," then wrote stories with long sentences with many commas. We read Céline's *Voyage au bout de la nuit* and wrote angry diatribes full of foulmouthed invective and poorly composed mash-ups. For Colette's *La vagabonde*, we pounded out lusty sex scenes involving petite French women. The Mathieus found these exercises ludicrous.

But I was more cheerful about it because it turned out I had a decent talent for aping other people's work. My French improved rapidly, if not for the most flattering reason: I was a hopeless mimic. Stick me with French people, and I begin to speak like a French person. Put me in a conversation with a Brit, and within moments I'm peppering my sentences with "rubbish" and "brilliant" and "at the end of day," a tendency ripe for ridicule.

Senior year, as soon as school broke for winter recess, I flew right back to the Mathieus for three weeks' vacation. I also went there directly after graduation, before heading to an internship in the South of France, and when that turned out to be a fiasco, I called Carole, asking to be rescued. "Quick—come to French mommy!" she replied, and I spun right around back to Paris again.

This time, I wasn't there to learn and I wasn't there to visit; I needed to make up the money I'd expected to earn at the failed internship. If you had no working papers, in the brutal parlance of the time, you had to find work *au noir*—literally "like a black person," or paid under the table. The expression was so widely used it was impossible to solicit job applications without it. The alternative was to let out a tangle of words (*hors du loi? sans papiers? illégalement?*) that would only persuade potential employers that you didn't speak French.

In the end, it was an American company, Häagen-Dazs, that was willing to pay me *au noir*; perhaps that was just their way. My new job title was *scoopeuse*.

All the aping of French writing and reading of French comic strips and chatting with the Mathieus had by this point led to a certain level of fluency. This was the first foreign language I'd successfully learned, and it went straight to my head. Once installed behind the counter, I adopted the singsongy cadence and snide attitude of the most Parisian of shop clerks. I greeted each customer with ferocity.

"*Bonjour! Qu'est-ce que vous désirez?*"

"*Oui! Vous voulez en cornet ou en pot?*"

All this with a rapid-fire Parisian delivery and a refusal to downshift into English for baffled tourists, which at the time I rationalized as far less condescending than the remedial English most shopkeepers reverted to when faced with the Obviously Not French. Even flavor titles like Peanut Butter Burst were rendered in a decisive French accent. The Americans who patronized our shop expressed open confusion at their silly *scoopeuse*. "What the hell are *pepites*?" they'd ask each other while I stared back in resolute French silence. What were they doing getting American ice cream in Paris anyway?

On busy days, the manager thrust a popsicle stand out into the square, which one of us had to man at our peril. A hardy band of Roma considered the square theirs and attacked whoever occupied that cart. Roma mothers would point us out to their children, demonstrating how to throw stray litter at our uniforms and accosting us with disagreeable shouts. Who knows what Häagen-Dazs had done to inspire the vitriol but, as the company's Place des Fontaines representative, I wanted to avoid getting garbage on the apron I was responsible for perfecting each morning. (Later, in an attempt to understand the Roma, I read Isabel Fonseca's devastating book *Bury Me Standing*, which explained the hardships the Roma have long endured. The title comes from a Roma expression, "Bury me standing, I've been on my knees all my life.")

Even in August, nearly emptied of Parisians, the city was my refuge. My Häagen-Dazs was near an enormous subterranean mall with one of the best branches of FNAC, a mega-multimedia store along the lines of Barnes & Noble. After work, I'd head into FNAC, where I'd rummage through the BDs and stare at the glossy white covers of the *livres de poche*, curious to see which American authors merited translation. I'd walk across to the Left Bank and explore the tiny bookshops of the rue des Écoles and the movie houses of the 6th arrondissement. The city devoted so much space to the things I cared about, I wanted to kiss the sidewalk in gratitude.

Paris became my regular escape hatch, the place I'd run off to whenever the cultural and intellectual and gut-level need arose. Over the next fifteen years, I would go to Paris more than a dozen times. (This isn't as obnoxious as it sounds: flights cost three hundred dollars round-trip and I slept on spare mattresses; it was a relatively cheap vacation.) And it was deeply therapeutic. I went there after a failed relationship; I went there after a failed job. I'd stay with the Mathieus, my thoughts paralleled in Claire Bretécher's *Les Frustrés* comic strips, marveling at how fully she captured the vicissitudes of my life, like a Frenchified Roz Chast. One summer, I read Barbara Tuchman's *A Distant Mirror* at the Mathieus' house outside Paris, from which I could visit the actual Château de Coucy, only a few towns away; this was life as it should be.

It was in Paris that I finally felt distant enough from the person I was in New York, the one who spent her twenties hustling away at marketing jobs while really wanting to be a writer, and comfortable enough to admit to anyone that maybe I actually was a writer. If there's any place on the planet where you can feel comfortable articulating an artistic or intellectual desire without feeling like a pretentious idiot (or at least more of a pretentious idiot than anyone else), surely it is Paris.

By the year 2000, I'd been freelancing for the *Economist* for several years, but the magazine had no bylines. Without my name inked permanently onto a piece of circulating paper, I didn't feel legit. I'd just quit my job at a media conglomerate to work on my first book; I was trying to write full-time for the first time in my life and I was nervous about the entire enterprise. One afternoon, my adoptive French sister, Juliette, and French brother, Paul, had friends over for lunch and we were crowded around the kitchen table. A friend of Paul's asked what I did for a living.

"*Je suis écrivain*," I ventured in a tentative voice. I had never said it before. In French, you don't say "I am a writer," you say, "I am writer," which gives the statement an even more boastful and pompous air. Writer, like poet or philosopher, isn't one of those job titles that rolls off the tongue in any language. The essayist Phillip Lopate once described the trepidation of declaring himself a writer for the first time. "I felt as though I were feigning a part, but what I would come to learn was that bluffing is an integral part of becoming a writer: you bluff and you bluff, until one day the world starts to treat you like a writer and you think (you are the last one to think it), 'Well maybe I actually am one,' still feeling mentally puny."

I did feel dangerously small, but under the veil of translation and with the distance from home and the immediate embrace of the Mathieus as a layer of protection, it was possible I had a case. Nobody knew that back home I wasn't *really* a writer, not yet. Nobody here in Paris thought I was obsessed with words. It was okay to devote hours to considering which book to read next, and to have the audacity to try writing one. Perhaps here I could pass.

"*Oh, là, là, Paméla est écrivain!*" Paul repeated in a mock haute Parisian accent when his friend looked impressed. But it was brotherly and affectionate, and Paul's eyes twinkled. He may have been making fun of me, but he was also proud. Most important, he believed me when I said it, which made it seem like it might even be true. I felt only slightly idiotic, but that may be the smartest, or at least safest, way to feel when you're starting out as a writer in this world.

CHAPTER 8

A Journey of One's Own

Books That Change Your Life

It's one thing to read books, quite another to presume to be involved in their creation. At Brown, a place swarming with smart and talented writers, to want to be a writer or to in some way participate in the literary world had meant facing a terrifying competition. Rather than risk failing at something, I did what so many college students at sea do: I aimed for something I didn't really want. The reward would be diminished, but so would the risk. I'd spent twenty-two years responding to fear with caution. Why stop now?

Sometimes it takes a book to jolt you out of where you are. It doesn't have to be a great book. Just the right book at the right moment, one that opens something up or exposes you to something new or somehow forces you to reexamine your life; the sustained and immersive experience of reading a book can do this in ways not even the best TV show or movie can. It can be altogether transformative.

In the spring of 1993 I needed that kind of book. It was my senior year in college, and I was in a University Career Services office, talking to a recruiter from Quaker Oats.

"Pleasantly sweet, yet tangy," I chirped with a smile, extolling the virtues of Cap'n Crunch cereal with Crunch Berries. And then I stopped.

In a moment of clarity, I saw myself from a bird's-eye view, self-conscious and in a stiff J.Crew suit reciting canned oratory about packaged goods. Look at that nervous young woman trying to persuade someone to let her peddle sugar-coated cereal to goggle-eyed children, kids who would surely be better off eating pretty much anything else. She was not the person I wanted to be. I felt a wash of nausea, as if I'd actually consumed an entire box of Crunch Berries. Was this what all the reading and studying and career planning had been for, the reason my parents had forked over tens of thousands of dollars for a fancy education?

Why *did* I want to work at Quaker Oats? That was the question the interviewer was asking and he needed an answer.

I had found one possible answer at the local bookstore, but it was to the wrong question. That question was one I'd been asking myself over the last few months, and it was even more intimidating. What if I *didn't* get a job, not at Quaker Oats, not anywhere? It was a realistic, and frightening, possibility. The economy was mired in a recession. I wasn't very good at interviewing. I didn't really want to do what I didn't really want to do, and it seemed the people interviewing me could tell.

The last time I'd openly admitted to wanting to be a writer was on an application for the Coca-Cola/Martin Luther King Scholarship senior year in high school; I'd won third prize. ("I would like to be a senator, both at the state and federal level. Also, I would like to be a writer—fiction and nonfiction.") I'd entered dozens such competitions to help supplement my financial aid package—I'd also won third place in the *Seventeen* magazine short-story contest. For that, my prize was a Brother word processor, useful because I couldn't afford a computer. After these decent but not stellar performances, I'd made college slightly cheaper but given up openly aiming for a life in letters.

The runner-up jobs, writing for a magazine or working at a publishing house, didn't pay enough for me to support myself, and I was scared to apply anyway. As for the money jobs, no matter how hard I tried to conform to corporate expectations, I didn't seem to be what they wanted. They could smell my ambivalence.

But one book suggested a tantalizing alternative: *A Journey of One's Own: Uncommon Advice for the Independent Woman Traveler* had been published just the year before by the spectacularly named Thalia Zepatos. "A teacher, spokeswoman, and heroine of sorts to a generation of travelers" (according to the *Seattle Times*), Zepatos had traveled to fifty countries by plane, train, donkey, camel, oxcart, bicycle, bus, truck, boat, and foot. Then she wrote a book urging other women to do the same. I should have been ingesting passages of *What Color Is Your Parachute?*, but I bought Zepatos's book instead.

A Journey of One's Own offered the life I wanted to be living if only I were a different person. I was nothing like Thalia Zepatos, heroine to a generation, rider of donkey and camel. But I wanted to be like her, to do what she had done, to go where she had gone, to have her sense of freedom and carefree yet purposeful indirection. I coveted her indifference to the narrow and directed path I'd followed, a path that was terrifying to veer off of.

In her introduction, Zepatos asked, "Why do we wait to travel? We wait until the time is right, until the car is paid off, until the kids are grown." None of those things were problems here. I hadn't even begun. Unlike many of my friends, I wasn't graduating college with a boyfriend. I didn't have kids; my plans were tethered to exactly no one. And I certainly didn't have a job. "We wait to feel secure and confident enough to go alone," Zepatos continued. Her soaring next paragraph felt like a direct challenge:

> One day I decided to stop waiting and start traveling. As a woman, I had frequently challenged the restrictions others had placed on what I could do. While traveling, I challenged the limits I had placed on myself. I got tired of the way my own fears restrained my ideas of where I could go, with whom and how.

You know that experience of reading thoughts you haven't yet articulated to yourself? I, too, was about to be trapped by my own fears into a future I didn't want. I was doing what was expected of me, though I wasn't sure where those expectations had come from or whose, precisely, they were. Now Thalia Zepatos was saying, Don't let that happen.

I had to get out of Quaker Oats. Back in the interview room, I looked up at the Cinnamon Life emissary, with his charcoal-gray poise and careful hair and targeted gaze. His fingers, complete with wedding band, clunky class ring, and manicured nails, drummed the desktop with just the teensiest note of impatience. Despite hours dissecting manuals on interview skills, I felt ill prepared—and, worryingly, inappropriate, as if I'd already done something that negatively impacted his bottom line.

"I like our cereal, too," my interrogator finally agreed with a chuckle. He stared at me with intention. "But really, why do you want to work for Quaker Oats?"

I had no idea.

"You're right," I said, beaten once and for all. "I don't actually want to work at Quaker Oats. I'm sorry to have wasted your time." I gathered my belongings and excused myself. On the way out of Career Services, I canceled my remaining appointments on the recruitment schedule.

It had been the honest answer. I did not want to work at Quaker Oats. I wanted to be a writer, which was impossible. I wanted to work in magazine or book publishing, but the starting salary at Farrar, Straus & Giroux was $14,500; a "good" editorial salary was $17,000, and I couldn't afford that. In those days, moving back in with your parents simply wasn't allowed. Moreover, my mother had divorced her second husband and moved into a one-bedroom apartment in the city. I'd never had a bedroom at my father's. Both of them literally didn't have room for me, which was frankly fine.

The trouble was finding an alternative. My bank account was nearly empty. Every check I'd gotten as a child had gone directly into college savings and now college was over. I'd worked on-campus jobs as part of my financial aid package, first helping fund-raise for the school's athletic programs from wealthy donors and then catering to prominent alumni and other dignitaries at luxury events on campus that rewarded them for their gifts. Both jobs demonstrated that in terms of money there were two worlds at college: the people who had it easy and the people who helped make those people's lives even easier. I didn't enjoy that second job, and the first wasn't right for me.

There was of course the option to stay in school. I'd had one other ambition before graduation, which was to get a graduate degree; I knew I wasn't done learning. I could keep reading, get a doctorate in history, and stay in school forever. My favorite history professor smiled sadly when I stated my intentions.

"Think about where you'd like to be after grad school," he said. "Because you won't be in New York. You won't be at a school like this. You will teach somewhere in Iowa, and not at the main state campus but at some small offshoot out in a pasture. And unless you have someone to pay for it, you will also owe thousands of dollars." It wasn't personal, he assured me. There just were no jobs. The period I was interested in—the world wars—wasn't fashionable in a grad school market held tight in the grip of deconstruction and post-Marxian analysis.

"You don't want to go to grad school," he said gently.

Was I really so predictable? Much as I loved New York, there was something depressing about going off to college only to have a professor tell you that you ought to turn around and go home. It was also depressing to think I couldn't somehow superstar my way through grad school into a tenure-track position. Perhaps my run of academic successes up to that point—the hard-earned grades, the coveted acceptance to Brown, the scholarships—had used up my lifelong share. Perhaps they didn't add up to that much anyway. (Third place, third place.)

I must have done something wrong. If a failed interview with

Quaker Oats was where my experiences had led, those experiences must have been fairly limited. Perhaps they hadn't been the right experiences.

Trudging down the main commercial drag on campus, I was plagued with doubt. How were you supposed to make a lifelong decision when you had so little experience? If you weren't fitting into the future this environment had created, perhaps a new environment was necessary.

And that's where *A Journey of One's Own* fit in. What Thalia Zepatos's book did was allow me to start an entirely new story for myself, one with no foreseeable ending. You could abandon the career rush altogether—not giving up, exactly, just opting out.

What I had to do, I decided, was challenge all of the assumptions and wrong-footed moves I'd made that led to that Quaker Oats interview. I'd do something that would quite possibly make me miserable. Maybe even *try* to do something that would make me miserable. I had made a few such moves before: joining the college rugby team because I was bad at sports and the gospel choir because I was an atheist who couldn't sing. But the field of risk now was much greater than an afternoon extracurricular activity. It was my life. It could end up being a terrible mistake.

But I couldn't help wondering: What would it be like to pick up and go somewhere else, somewhere I had zero interest in, a place with a different religion, a different ethnicity, an unknown language? A place where I would be in the minority. A place where I knew no one. Somewhere you couldn't go about your usual routine, diligently checking off boxes and getting things done. A place that challenged each moment of your day: no morning dose of coffee, no *New York Times* over a toasted sesame bagel, no level-six StairMaster workout, no dispiriting crush on the guy in the next cubicle.

I could go somewhere where none of these activities were even possible, some remote country, a place Cap'n Crunch had never sailed. To me, a history major of the most occidental school, the world was Weimar Germany, Charles de Gaulle, and the Gettysburg Address. I had to get out of there. I needed a place where the mind-set—the whole philosophy—was different, a non–Judeo-Christian culture where each of my moments would be challenged. Asia, I decided. I knew nothing about the entire continent beyond the grossest generalizations. I had never been part of those students who became enamored of Japanese design or wrote papers about Mao Zedong. I hated Benihana.

Reading the motivational passages in *A Journey of One's Own* ("Women actively explore the inner as well as the outer landscapes of our journeys—we don't just take in the sights, we are changed by the things we see and the people we meet"), I hatched a plan for someone else, someone who wasn't quite me but, rather, the Thalia-like person I wanted to be. Maybe instead of just reading about other women's stories, I could become a person worthy of my own.

Thalia Zepatos wouldn't have wound up at Quaker Oats. Thalia Zepatos, whoever she was (she is now a marriage equality activist, according to the Internet), had lived in a tribal village in the Golden Triangle. If only I knew what the Golden Triangle was, I might live there too.

What *A Journey of One's Own* started, other books helped along, including the tiny, blurry photographs in the Lonely Planet guides at the college bookstore. Bearded men descending on the Ganges, saffron-robed monks floating in the rain, betel-lipped women folded over sodden fields. What were they thinking about, what were their days like, what did they want to do with their lives? I read these books, marked them down in Bob (yes, travel guides count), and fantasized about their contents before drifting off to sleep. One of these countries would be my destination.

By process of elimination—Nepal had no jobs, Indonesia was too volatile, India was impractical—the answer became Thailand. For its Buddhism, its jungles, its relative prosperity and stability, and, most important, its unfamiliarity. I knew nobody in Thailand nor did I know anyone who'd ever been there. (American college students who backpacked in those days tended to favor Nepal or Latin America over Southeast Asia; Thailand wasn't on the circuit.) I knew nothing about Theravada Buddhism, orchid cultivation, or the language. I had eaten Thai food only once and had never even seen *The King and I*. I had neither preconceptions nor expectations.

After the Quaker Oats debacle, I took the decisive next step of purchasing a shiny copy of *Fodor's Exploring Thailand* for a steep $21.95. I clutched it to my chest like a Girl Scout pin, daydreaming about possible encounters with people based on the book I was carrying. It's the perennial reader's fantasy, the hope that the right book will magically spur strangers into intimate and telling conversations or elevate your standing in the eyes of people you already know.

"What's with the book?" someone, perhaps a professor or a desired acquaintance or an old boyfriend, would ask in this imagined scenario.

"Oh, this?" I'd respond blithely, relishing their fascination.

"I'm moving to Thailand." Nobody I knew did such a thing. All the go-getters were going into investment banking and consulting; the arty types often relied on trust funds; the brainy ones and preprofessionals escaped into grad school. Everyone else scrambled, desperate not to be left behind. They had plans.

This was before gap years were in vogue. This was before the Internet shrunk the world and everyone was just a text away. Letters traveled slowly and international calls cost a fortune. In 1993, tossing your college degree into the wind and moving to a remote town in a third-world country with no job was the equivalent of someone today flinging his iPhone into the sea and joining a religious cult in rural Kentucky where everyone speaks Esperanto and reassembles old Hyundais for money. It made no sense, and it probably meant something was wrong with you.

Well, I'd show them. Summoning the heroes previously met only in books, I began to fancy myself a kind of female Joseph Conrad, departing from my native land, traveling over distant seas, defying convention or at least the expectations of my classmates, professors, and family members. This was my way of joining the Merchant Marine. The more I defended my decision to other people, several of whom thought I was throwing away a promising career, the more I started to believe in it. I told my mom, I told Career Services, and I told my roommates, all of whom had secured smart jobs in major cities. I told my father, who liked to read about the Far East in Paul Theroux's books and watch it on the Discovery Channel; for him, travel was something done from a recliner.

"That's wonderful, Pammy," he said. "I'm not paying for your plane ticket."

Now that I'd told everyone, announcing my plans repeatedly,

a retraction would have meant an inconceivable embarrassment. I sold my 1985 Honda and bought a nonrefundable one-way ticket to Chiang Mai, a small city of 150,000 people ("really an overgrown village," according to the books) nestled in the hills of northern Thailand.

By March, "What are you going to do next year?" became the standard campus greeting, replacing "How did the interview go?" Everyone was telling each other what offers they'd taken, salaries, cities, significant others, where she was, where he was, where they were all going. They were moving along.

"Really, *Thailand*?" people would say when I shared my vision. (Sometimes—I am sorry to report—"*Taiwan*?")

"Maybe for two or three years," I'd reply casually, saying something vague about adventure and opportunity and the expectations of women and why the hell not. I would free myself from material possessions while I was at it, packing a single suitcase, minimal clothing, a few books, and, of course, Bob. I cut off my hair and colored the remaining blond pixie dark brown. I willed myself to feel tougher about the fact that I hadn't had the guts to go for what I'd really wanted.

"You're so brave!" people would finally say, probably for lack of anything else. Perhaps they were writing me off. I didn't necessarily feel like I could take credit for the move. It seemed more like 5 percent of me had made a firm decision and dragged the unwitting other 95 percent along. I had no idea whether a new lifestyle would make me feel more fulfilled or whether it would prove I'd been happy all along and merely unappreciative. This wasn't something that could be figured out by reading a book. Sometimes you need to go out and search for the answer. But it took a book to push me along.

CHAPTER 9

Anna Karenina

Heroines

Every girl has her heroines. Mine were the ones who had motivated me in biographies, ever since I was eight years old, curled up in my favorite part of the children's library, the back wall where, neatly arranged in alphabetical order, were my sacred lives: Abigail Adams, Louisa May Alcott, Clara Barton . . .

If I wanted to know what other girls my age had done and where it led them, I consulted these books, these people who had already lived well, for instruction. I listened to them, tried to follow in their footsteps and learn from their mistakes. In their stories, and with the wisdom of hindsight, any awkward childhood encounter or passing trauma could be seen as a necessary step toward a greater future.

Poor misunderstood Helen Keller needed that moment of

frustration by the water pump. Jane Addams had to suffer her childhood illness and the death of her mother when she was only two years old. I'd never be as good as Florence Nightingale or Dolley Madison (the name Pamela, which my mother had chosen because it was the title of the first English novel, also meant "selfish," my *Baby Name Guide* cruelly informed me), but I could try. Maybe the kid at recess telling me the flood was over when my hand-me-down Lee jeans were too short was a hardship I needed to suffer.

Bookish girls tend to mark phases of their lives by periods of intense character identification. For almost a century and a half, we've fluctuated between seasons of Amy and Meg and Jo, imagining ourselves alternately the prettiest or the eldest or the most ambitious of the Little Women. But every girl who aspired to become a writer fancied herself as strong and independent Jo.

When I was ten, I aimed to be as clever as Nancy Drew, resolving any dilemma with purpose and grit. On the cusp of junior high, I was turned on to horse-girl books by my friend Ericka, who actually rode horses. (I was too scared.) She got me involved in a series starring a girl named Francesca, my next role model. Both Ericka and Francesca had long, shiny chestnut-brown hair that was nothing like my mess of dirty blond. Horse girls were strong and fearless and altruistic; they knew how to jump.

Schoolgirls of the seventies muddled through childhood in the guise of one Judy Blume heroine or another (Sally J. Freedman occupying a central role), just the way girls today work through Hermione and Tris and Katniss Everdeen. If something happened to one of them that had happened to you, it meant you weren't a freak; there was precedent. And if you could find out what they did about it, you might find your own solution, or at least learn what not to do. Through them, you could envisage an alternate existence, heroic or tragic or just more interesting than your own.

In the fall of 1993, at age twenty-two, I chose Anna Karenina. I was living in a foreign country, with little purpose other than to put myself in the way of challenge. I'd just moved to the outskirts of Chiang Mai, a small city in northern Thailand, and Anna Karenina offered an appropriate parallel. She, too, was isolated from her people. She, too, acted independently and wasn't necessarily rewarded for it. She was a modern woman bucking expectations, and, at least I liked to believe, so was I.

I had a few thousand dollars in savings and a suitcase. My Thai, feebly informed by the GI Prep Course Language Tapes I'd listened to the summer before my move—"Where is the air-field?"; "Is it a comedy or a tragedy?"—was not a bankable asset. I didn't know anyone and I didn't have a job.

At least I'd picked the right country. I was thrilled to be in Thailand and dazzled by Thai culture, with its gentle appreciation of aesthetics, its spicy cuisine, and its reverence for tradition. I loved the charmingly antiquated cinematic tribute to the king, which played before the feature film in every movie house. I just needed to figure out what, if any, kind of heroine I could be in this new and very strange scenario, and then discover my storyline.

After a period of fitful acclimating to a world in which I understood approximately 4 percent of what was going on around me, I managed to land part-time work teaching English, French, and history at various schools. I found a language tutor and I found a new home on a place called the Farm—more of an untended fruit orchard than an agricultural endeavor—in a small, elevated teak house with an outdoor kitchen and a bare pipe poking out of the ground for a sink. It felt authentically Thai rather than tourist-friendly, and I even found a Thai roommate, a minuscule college student named Nai Noi. Or she found me.

Nai Noi was a "play" name meaning Sir Small; her real name, Acheeraya, meant "genius." All Thais have an official given name, used infrequently, and a descriptive play name, like Sweet or Fat or Water Heart (which meant generous). Though she was an English major at Chiang Mai University, Nai Noi was unlike anyone I'd encountered in college. She was in her sixth year after changing majors, and she still had two years to go. She seemed to never read any of the assigned books nor did she want to read mine, rarely did homework, and didn't once ask me for help. Having dated a student on the Princeton in Asia program a couple of years earlier, she was completely fluent in English anyway.

We weren't alone. There were scorpions in our backyard and a large geckolike creature called a Toogaeh who lived under the eave of the roof and croaked out "Too gaeh, too gaeh, too gaeh . . . gaeh," the final syllable sounding a note of weary melancholia, every night at exactly ten thirty, poking out its head to bid us good night. When I woke up my first morning there and instinctively grabbed the glass of water I'd set by the book on my nightstand, my hand tingled. I half opened an eye. Just inches from my face, my hand was pulsating within a swarm of black ants. "Get out of our water," they said.

The ants had entered through the open wooden slats of the wall and marched in single file toward the glass alongside my bed, behind my toes, and over my pillow before plunging into my glass, pleased with the welcoming beverage I'd provided. I can't say I welcomed them in return. It was hard to read in bed at night surrounded by the incessant movement of small shiny black creatures and even harder to fall asleep knowing of their relentless forward march, but there was no way to get rid of them in a room with open walls. They distracted me. I was reminded of a cruelty my brother Roger inflicted on me on a regular basis when we were kids: I'd be peacefully reading in bed, when, as the mood struck, he'd fling open my bedroom door, which didn't have a proper latch, and wiggle his hand through; the peripheral movement made concentrating on the page impossible. Getting up to chase him out only compounded the interruption.

But what could be done? Killing bugs wasn't Buddhist. If I asked Nai Noi to dispel the encroaching wilderness, she would daintily pick up the spiders that hung vertically from the shower ceiling and escort them one by one outdoors. They always came back. I learned to wrap my hand in toilet paper before flushing the toilet; its handle was inevitably teeming with ants.

It was harder to acclimate to the giant water bug who lived behind the toilet bowl. He'd come out late at night as I sat there, determinedly confronting me from the puddled floor. (Thai bathrooms did not have separate shower stalls so the floor was always wet and often sticky.) The water bug, more like a New York City rat than a cockroach, was so large you could see into his eyes and read his defiance. After flushing I would catapult off the toilet in Olympian fashion, clearing the water bug, and, panting heavily, run back to bed and my awaiting ants.

One night I snapped. Not fully aware of what I was doing, I grabbed *Anna Karenina* off my bed and brought it down with all my might on the water bug. I smote him. Turning on the spidery showerhead, I let the bloody remains swirl around in a wet mess until he was nothing more than a brackish veneer. I wiped the crushed limbs off my book cover. My heroine had come to the rescue.

When I looked up, there was Nai Noi, surveying me with her enormous Buddhist eyes. Murderer. One week later, sitting on the toilet, there was a second confrontation. A new water bug, even mightier than the first, was standing directly before me. I swear I could hear him say, "My name is Inigo Montoya. You killed my father. Prepare to die."

These emissaries from the natural world were telling me something: I wasn't really cut out for the Farm. I loved living there, but not as my former urbanite self, as someone new, someone who did things I didn't do. In Thailand, I climbed a mountain, learned to motorcycle, and accidentally ate durian, the dread "stinky fruit." I crossed the border into forbidden Burma. I even ended up riding a donkey and a camel, Thalia Zepatos–style, and an elephant too. Being off the path didn't always come easily. Sometimes I would ride around town on my motorbike, running unnecessary errands, just to feel like I had someone to meet or somewhere to go. I'd stop at a newsstand to read as much of the *International Herald Tribune* as I possibly could on the rack without feeling shamed into buying it, something I'd budgeted to do twice a week, making sure to get the weekend edition, with its movie and book reviews. I'd head to the library at the Association of American Alumni, where they had three-week-old copies of the Sunday *New York Times*. At night, I read my comfort books, hauled across the globe from New York. Hello, home culture.

As much as I was getting out of the experience, I wasn't always sure Thailand wanted me there. One night on my way home to the Farm, an angry water buffalo came careening down my lane of the highway, against traffic, bent on mowing me down. It felt like an unfortunate metaphor, the natural world telling me, "Watch out. You're going the wrong way." On another occasion, a full-size municipal bus turned straight onto me as I puttered en route to a local guesthouse for a twenty-cent passion fruit shake. My motorbike was thrown against a telephone pole, the front tire somehow landing parallel to the road, squashed beneath one of the bus's front wheels. Everyone on board was abuzz at the site of a damaged foreigner, pointing and gaping out the windows. Physically, I was fine. But I felt like an idiot for ending up under a bus, making a spectacle of myself in front of a crowd of people who surely knew better.

My very presence in Thailand felt inherently offensive despite a constant effort to avoid offense. I didn't tell anyone, for example, what I really thought about ghosts, which Thais take seriously, building small wooden "spirit houses" outside every residence and office building so the ghosts will elect to stay there rather than wander into human territory. Despite such precautions, ghosts occasionally do come inside and cause trouble. Spring semester, a ghost moved into the dorm room of one of Nai Noi's classmates, Oi (Sugarcane). "The first night the ghost just lay quietly in the corner, but on the second night, she leaned over my bed," Oi confided. "She was crying and whispering my name." Apparently, that's all it took for Oi and her roommate to get the hell out of there, leaving the ghost with a spacious double to herself. Oi temporarily moved into our house until the university could relocate her into a ghost-free dorm. The only one who didn't seem understanding was me, and I was teased for my obtuseness on the matter.

I regularly found new ways to draw attention to my ignorance. For weeks, I helpfully told shopkeepers who were tending to other customers, "Don't worry—I can wait." The inevitable response was baffled silence. It turned out I was using the wrong tone and was in fact saying, "Don't worry, I can penis." On another occasion, as I gathered my clothes to have them cleaned and folded by a local laundry, as I'd been doing since I'd arrived in Thailand, Nai Noi recoiled in horror.

"You can't, you can't . . ." she said in a strangled voice. I stared at her, awaiting enlightenment. "Underwear," she finally sputtered. "You can't give them your underwear."

My underwear? I knew my underwear wasn't clean at that moment. But what I didn't know was that in Thailand, women's underwear is *never* clean. It is by its very nature a foul and despoiled thing, and can never, ever be handled by anyone other than the woman who wears it. Women's underwear was dangerous just as women were dangerous—helpless and yet dangerous—and helplessly dangerous.

What kind of heroine was I, anyway? In my own small-scale Anna Karenina style, I, too, was trying to act independently but inadvertently defying social norms. Everywhere I went, people asked about my husband. *Where is he?*, they needed to know, with the implied, *How could he have let you come here by yourself?* I lied about him since he didn't exist, even contemplating wearing a fake wedding ring, as many women did while abroad. But I didn't want to pretend I was something I wasn't, and I didn't appreciate the suggestion that a wedding ring made me inherently less unnerving. A wedding ring also seemed to shut off any prospect of future romance, which I held on to with dwindling hope.

My Vronsky was nowhere to be found. Moving abroad, I'd expected to meet other young college graduates keen on adventure. Instead I met people fleeing bad marriages, on the prowl for subservient Thai wives or underage sex partners, pedophiles and misfits, missionaries and teachers who hadn't succeeded at teaching at home. Everyone had something to escape and someone to exploit. One night after a Thai kickboxing match, a bunch of us went to a bar catering to expats and were immediately surrounded by prostitutes. They dove into the laps of every middle-aged white man, giggling and fawning with sly expertise. My presence was superfluous. Just being there felt like its own kind of racist acquiescence and degradation.

Still I held on to hope that I might meet some like-minded fellow American traveler, pitifully encouraged by a psychic monk who offered to read my palm during a Thai lesson one afternoon. It was difficult to read women's hands, he explained, because much of a good palm reading involved touch, and monks were forbidden to touch women. By his estimate, about 30 percent of the available information would be lost. Still, he leaned forward, peering at my outstretched hand. I was, he pronounced, an impatient, critical, and stubborn person. "Your life will require intense effort in the next few years," he told me. My stomach, he emphasized, was in horrible shape; I ought to see a doctor.

"You are intelligent and artistic," he continued, perhaps in response to my grimace. "You work with your hands, but not manual labor. You do the work of an artist." Now *this* was more like it. I longed for a lover, he said delicately, yet would not find one for a long time.

"But when you do"—he smiled, curling a long pinkie nail in front of my nose—"it will be magic. No effort. Done!"

Just not yet. Everyone else I worked with at the International School seemed to be getting busy. Clive and Neil, an expat couple from Australia who taught elementary students, fed their bickery relationship with a parade of outside stimulation. Clive was bitter about being a teacher in Thailand when he was meant to be in the theater in Sydney, bitter because no matter how many he tried, he didn't actually like Thai men, and bitter because, with his squishy physique and parsimoniousness, he wasn't their type either. This was not a problem for his partner Neil, who looked sixteen, taught fourth grade, and liked to pick up teenage boys after work.

Beyond these activities, neither Clive nor Neil had much interest in the Thai people. Clive refused to learn the language because, he declared, "I doubt they'd have anything to tell me that couldn't be relayed by someone in English." Thailand, Clive liked to say, had no culture because it lacked a literary tradition. There were no Thai novels written before the late twentieth century, he informed me—a sign, he declared, of a fundamental absence of imagination.

I set out to find Thai literature, if only to refute him. Not much had been translated for the literary appetites of Westerners. In an English-language bookshop ten hours south in Bangkok (there were none in Chiang Mai), I picked up a copy of Khamsing Srinawk's *The Politician and Other Stories*. Srinawk, a writer from the impoverished northeast, was one of the best-known writers in the country. A journalist turned short-story writer, he benefited from a brief period of press freedom in the late fifties, when his stories began appearing in local newspapers. He had traveled abroad in the sixties as the recipient of a Time-Life grant; later, he became politically active and was exiled and banned before returning in the eighties.

Srinawk's work, often satirical in nature, gave voice to the Thai peasant class. Just the year before my arrival in Thailand, the National Culture Commission named him the National Artist of Thailand in literature. There *was* Thai literature; Clive just didn't know about it. The limits of his curiosity exasperated me. I made a heavy notation of *The Politician and Other Stories* in my Book of Books in frustration.

It had been a long time since I'd hung out with someone my age, from a similar background, someone to whom I wouldn't have to explain myself and all my references, someone who was inspired by the same stories. Of course, I had sought precisely this scenario by moving to Thailand in the first place. Living there was a constant exhilaration and provocation; I just hadn't realized how tiring that would be. My main release was on paper— books and Bob and letters home, long missives I sent to my mother called Pamograms, which she photocopied and mailed to a list of friends and family.

In my Pamograms and in my mind, I tried to envision myself a noble heroine in a grand and epic novel culminating in the realization of some larger purpose. If not Anna Karenina, then some equally romantic but less suicidal figure. Any morning could be the dawn of a new narrative, one tailored to that day's circumstance, something that would offer, if not a happy ending, then at least a better story line. You could assume the character of whatever novel or biography you were reading at the moment, create your own, or attempt to alter yourself to suit any relevant ambitions. "Today, I'll be the more intrepid type," I'd tell myself upon waking, and proceed through the day like a character from a completely different story.

Over the years, I had developed a related habit of narrating my every move aloud, occasionally in the third person. "There she goes for the five-to-eleven shift," I'd mutter on my way to work. "Perhaps tonight she'll have rice pilaf for dinner." Mostly I yammered away in the plain old first person: "I'll just swing open the door of the car," I informed my best friend, Ericka, while visiting her at Wesleyan freshman year. "Then I'll get back in and drive up I-95. I should be there before dark."

"Stop it!" she yelled. I'd been doing this all weekend, apparently. "Stop narrating your every move! It's unbelievably annoying."

Oh my God she was right. I think I'd been annoyed, too, I just hadn't realized that I was the problem. From that day forward, I tried hard to keep the narration to myself, and to a minimum. Narrating your life necessarily means holding it at a certain distance. There's a risk to reading your life more than actually living it.

But I still unconsciously broke my days down into stories—tailoring haphazard sequences of events into neater narratives, ones with beginnings, middles, and ends circulating in my head like a private polyphonic novel. You could sketch out characters, editing as you went, predicting upcoming plot points, and then cleaning it up afterward. You could take full advantage of *l'esprit de l'escalier*, making everything just a little more clever than it actually was.

After dinner, enveloped by my ants, I'd plunge back into *Anna Karenina* and try to locate myself within Anna's story. Feeling unloved and unexcited by the relationship possibilities around me, I lived vicariously through Anna's mad affair with Vronsky, her desire and abandon filling the void where a boyfriend might have belonged. Her story expanded on my own, enriching and filling out the parts that felt missing. When you're young and single, infidelity is more opportunity than tragedy, and the pain of abandoning a child is unimaginable. Perhaps you'd read the book differently if you were newly married, finding it scandalous and wrong, or after you've been married for a time, at which point it might once again make you swoon but for different reasons. For me in that place and at that time, *Anna Karenina* was incredibly seductive, Anna's story adding a tinge of romance to round out the coarser aspects of my life abroad. Pitching myself onto a train track held zero appeal. I nonetheless wished I could be just a little more like my heroine.

CHAPTER 10

Swimming to Cambodia

The Company of Narrators

The friends I made living in Thailand were friends of circumstance—Angela, a yellow-haired English minister's daughter who wore brightly colored jewelry and said things like "faffy" and "grotty"; Brad, a fiftysomething history teacher from Hawaii who lived with a Thai teenager; Alma, a Swedish backpacker I hung out with on the beach, seemingly the only other solo girl on Ko Phi Phi for the holidays. Each provided a companionship of convenience; we probably never would have crossed paths at home, and if we had, we'd have each swiftly moved on. Here, I clung to them.

It would have been great to have had a real friend to travel with. It would have been even better to have had a real boyfriend to travel with. Instead, when I decided to go to Cambodia in the

spring of 1994 for the Cambodian New Year celebration, I had
Tyler. A former navy sailor, Tyler was the smartest and worldliest
American I'd met in Chiang Mai and my most recent companion of last resort. He was handsome in a mean and careless all-
star way, one of those guys who winked at plain women on the
street knowing it would make them blush. I couldn't have been
less interested in him romantically, which was saying something, since what I really could have used at that point was
romance. But that didn't seem to be Tyler's core strength anyway.
While stationed in the Philippines, he'd met, married, and abandoned a local woman after he couldn't get a Catholic divorce. He
then moved to Chiang Mai, where he rented a two-story wooden
house on the outskirts, turning the ground floor into an English-
language classroom. I chose not to inquire about his current love
life, but Tyler otherwise seemed relatively respectful of the local
population; his Thai was impeccable, and having developed a serious book habit during long, tedious hours on a submarine, he read
ambitiously in both Thai and English. If nothing else, we could
talk about literature together, and we did.

The most noteworthy thing about Tyler was the way he peed at
night. His toilet was located on the first floor of the house, a steep
and narrow staircase away from his upstairs bedroom. To avoid a
precarious descent in the dark of night down what was more a
ladder than a flight of stairs, he'd rigged a long plastic tube from
the first-floor toilet up the side of the house to the window of his
second-floor bedroom. At night, he'd simply release into the plastic tube and the runoff would make its way into the bowl. Tyler's
system, alas, did not accommodate women.

He was kind of a solo operator generally. Though he and I
didn't know each other well, we managed to find something to

fight about while waiting for our flight to Phnom Penh. Before boarding, we mutually decided to go our separate ways. My travels in Asia were too precious to be compromised by bad company.

"You can take the hostel," I said to Tyler at the airport; we'd reserved a room with two beds in the city's tiny backpacker ghetto. "I'll find somewhere else." This was easier said than done. It was early days in Cambodia's tourism revival and accommodations were hard to come by. The nascent tourist industry hadn't been helped when, three months prior to my trip, a professor from the University of Texas was kidnapped and killed by rogue Khmer Rouge fighters while she was visiting a temple outside Angkor Wat. Phnom Penh, the capital, was still dominated by UN forces and NGOs; the Khmer Rouge, who had been deposed more than a decade earlier, had yet to go on trial for crimes against humanity. There was only one luxury hotel in the entire country, a gleaming Sofitel for people of note; everyone else scattered into the remaining run-down establishments.

By sheer luck I wound up at the Renakse, an elegantly dilapidated French colonial hotel directly across from the Royal Palace. It was a step up from my usual grubby guesthouse, but I wanted to avoid bumping into Tyler within the cluster of budget accommodations. The Renakse, as it happened, was the prime hangout for a kind of expat very different from those populating Chiang Mai. Instead of missionaries and sex tourists, there were academics, artists, and nonprofit workers from Europe and the United States. So *here* were the people I'd been fruitlessly searching for abroad.

Despite parting ways with my ostensible traveling companion and making that departure much easier, I soon found good company. Based on title alone, I'd picked up a copy of *Swimming to Cambodia* by Spalding Gray, the theater director, monologist, and author, and begun reading it on the plane. Whenever I travel, I try to pack at least three times as many books as can be expected to read, so as to always have on hand something that fits my mood at a given moment. I would load these books in my backpack, and then, unless they were truly disappointing, I would haul them back. Reading was so much a part of any journey that I hated to leave my Book of Books out, preferring to watch the accumulation of titles in its pages signal a trip well traveled—it meant I had plenty of time on trains and buses, and good reading lamps in my hotels. But Bob usually didn't come with me; as soon as I would get home, I copied the titles and authors into his pages, the more, the better. This marked the end of every voyage, making it complete.

Especially when I chose the right book. It's hard to describe the intensity of emotion reading *Swimming to Cambodia*, Gray's monologue about his experiences playing a small role in the movie *The Killing Fields*. But it was immediate and all-consuming. Spalding Gray was my first literary crush.

There was no romance in this fervor, but rather a sense of total and complete identification. True, Spalding Gray was a New England Protestant who'd spent years working in avant-garde theater in Soho, and I was a near-unemployed college grad from Long Island. I didn't share Gray's struggles with drinking or his depression or the legacy of a suicidal mother. But I'd never, in reading a personal narrative, felt such a close affinity with a writer; it was as if we viewed the world through a shared lens. I found funny what he found funny and sad what he found sad. When I read him, I felt like I appreciated what he wrote in the way he wanted to be appreciated, and that he would have appreciated that.

Like me, Spalding was a compulsive narrator. That's what led to his odd job of monologuing and one-man theater, and to writing his stories down in book form. "Stories seem to fly out of me and stick," he explained in the preface to *Sex and Death to the Age 14*. "So I never wonder whether, if a tree falls in the forest, will anyone hear it. Rather, who will tell about it?" He began telling stories in college, when he got into a habit of recounting his day to his fellow employees at the Katharine Gibbs School, where he worked at night. Later, he told them to his girlfriend: "It felt as if I was peeling them off and dropping them in her lap so I could breathe again." Yes.

What was so impressive about Spalding's stories was that *he didn't have to make them up*. The events he described actually happened and he hadn't sought them out. "I saw vivid stories coming at me from the outside," he explained. Moreover, he was—or at least he came across as—unsparingly honest. Even when he embellished, he did it for dramatic effect and not to make himself come across better. It wasn't that he didn't have insecurities—he did, otherwise I never would have been able to relate to him—but his way of overcoming them or at least dealing with them was to storify and share them. He was doing what I only wished I could do.

Just reading Spalding seemed to magically forge connections to like-minded people. After noticing me reading *Swimming to Cambodia* over breakfast at the Renakse one morning, a documentary filmmaker staying down the hall asked me to join him for coffee. His previous projects had included work with the makers of *The Killing Fields*, and now he was making a film about land mines for the PBS series *Nova*. At the time, Cambodia had one land mine for every seven inhabitants.

We talked about *Swimming to Cambodia* and William Shawcross's *Sideshow*, which I'd recently read, and then, as if these books gained me passage, he invited me to join him and his friends on a boat they chartered on the Mekong River every Friday afternoon.

Also on board was Connie, a scholar of ancient Chinese poetry at Lehigh; a stunning American businesswoman named Heather who'd made a fortune in China while simultaneously getting a PhD from MIT; an anthropologist, also named Heather, who'd been working at the Sackler Museum in Beijing; Lindsay, a corporate lawyer from San Francisco who was assisting the Cambodian government to create laws related to women's issues; an unidentified gray-haired man who spoke with authority about everything from the kooky Vietnamese cult religion Caodaism (subjects of worship: Victor Hugo, Sun Yat-sen, and Winston Churchill) to the origins of the Vietnam War. And there was me.

The first few minutes were awkward as my fellow passengers introduced themselves in terms of their respective achievements. Then they asked what I did and I said something nebulous about working in Thailand. I tried hard to act like a legitimate participant in the conversation until Lindsay the Lawyer challenged me on my first attempt to seem like a grown-up. ("What do you mean exactly by 'matriarchal'? How is Cambodian society 'matriarchal'?" "Um, I overheard a tour guide say so?") I quickly downshifted to thoughtful nods. They may in fact have found me interesting as a Gen Xer living in Thailand, but at the time, I thought they saw me as just a kid.

I tagged along for drinks afterward at the Foreign Correspondents Club, where we were met with a scene straight out of Somerset Maugham, complete with enormous spinning fans on the ceiling and a long wooden bar. Everyone knew everyone else from earlier newspaper stints in Hong Kong or Singapore. Reporters and published academics swarmed the place. By comparison, I had written a few Pamograms and some well-received college papers.

For years, Spalding Gray remained the object of my literary fantasies. The authors I'd been obsessed with as a teenager either had been long dead or were stratospherically out of reach, but Spalding was different. He was alive, and while he was famous in his way, meeting him didn't feel entirely outside the realm of possibility; our worlds could conceivably coincide off the page. When I moved back to New York and lived in the East Village in the mid-nineties, it seemed fated that I would encounter him on my walk to work.

Part of me couldn't help but believe that once he knew who I was deep down, he would understand that we were meant to be friends. *I think about life the same way,* I wanted him to know. *I just haven't done anything with it.* I, too, was obsessed with Cambodia. I, too, had spent time on a beach in Thailand. Spalding had been to a meditation retreat and had seen gyrating testicles on the wall when he tried to meditate; I had thought about trying to meditate but hadn't because I was sure something would have distracted me, though probably not naked balls on the wall. Whatever happened, I'd tell him all about it.

Walking through his Soho neighborhood, I would plot our inevitable encounter, though whatever opening gambit I used (and I played out many in my head), it came across as fumbling and desperate:

"Hey, Spalding—huge fan of your work."

"Spalding Gray! Sorry to be so direct, but I really think we should be friends. Would you like to have lunch?"

It never happened. I walked through his neighborhood to

work for three years and attended every one of his shows in New York. Finally, in 1999, I went to a book signing and made a fawning and garbled confession. He signed my copy of *Morning, Noon and Night*, "To Pamela, THE STALKER." When he committed suicide in 2004, I not only missed the books he'd never write and the friendship we'd never know, I'd lost a kindred spirit.

During my two weeks in Cambodia, Spalding was still very much alive. He accompanied me to Siem Reap, where I otherwise had the deserted temples of Angor Wat to myself; this was before the temples were overrun with tour buses. When I had to run out of a temple to escape a local maintenance worker who had used an obscene gesture to suggest we fornicate in the soggy ruins, Spalding did the kindness of turning the episode into an amusing anecdote.

His wry humor lent levity and perspective to everything. I felt his presence when I foolishly paid a teenage boy to take me to the gruesome Killing Fields on the back of his motorbike (it's not as if there were cabs) and as I walked through the muddy, bone-ridden site. His wise, sardonic, yet deeply empathetic voice described everything I saw, inflecting my own. With Spalding by my side, even the darkest excursions became immeasurably richer and more droll. He was what every travel writer should be—a companion.

But the opposite can happen with a narrator, as I learned on a monthlong trip to Vietnam, another side trip I made while living in Thailand. Bookwise, I thought I had come ready. My Book of Books bore the telltale signs that peppered its pages before any trip: title after title about somewhere else. I'd gotten a brand-new updated *Lonely Planet Vietnam* and sped my way through a series of war-lit titles: Philip Caputo's *A Rumor of War*, Michael Herr's *Dispatches*, Le Ly Hayslip's harrowing memoir *When*

Heaven and Earth Changed Places and its follow-up, *Child of War, Woman of Peace*. I felt terrible about America's role in the Vietnam War, and even though I hadn't been around at the time, I was ready to make penance for all of it.

After paying my dues during a harrowing visit to the Museum of American War Crimes in Ho Chi Minh City, I moved on from the war into contemporary travelogue. Unfortunately, in doing so, I chose the wrong book, Justin Wintle's *Romancing Vietnam*. Wintle, a dyspeptic, Oxford-educated British journalist, also wanted to leave the war behind; he'd spent three months traveling the country in an attempt to uncover what he deemed the real Vietnam—its treatment of artists, its religious sects, its political heritage—but not surprisingly, the tightly controlled government rebuffed his reportorial efforts.

Most books and movies about Vietnam (*The Deer Hunter*, *Full Metal Jacket*, *Apocalypse Now*), Wintle complained, came from a distinctly American point of view. They didn't take into account the experiences of the people whose war they were in. Even when these movies criticized the war or the United States, he wrote, Vietnam was just a "testing ground where all the hallowed shibboleths of America are blown apart." This was the kind of anti-American critique that might have been palatable coming from other Americans; coming from a smug Brit like Wintle it was intolerable.

Wintle's attitude didn't improve. Despite his stated intent to get at the real Vietnam, on the page at least, he was chauvinistic and, for a journalist, oddly incurious. As one reader noted in an Amazon review, "What we get . . . reads at times like the memoirs of a fraternity boy: drinking, beautiful women, more drinking, more beautiful women." It felt like imitation Redmond O'Hanlon, without the fine prose and sense of humor. At one point, when offered female "companionship," Wintle triumphantly crowed, "Eat your heart out, Betty Friedan. A right gobsmack for Madame Greer."

This was my traveling companion. His snide voice infiltrated my own, sullying the landscape with his cynicism, making me feel like yet another ugly American and, worse, one in the company of an elitist Englishman. I'd landed in Ho Chi Minh City during Tet, the Vietnamese New Year celebration, a month after the United States lifted its embargo, which in travelers' terms was already too late. Those who were there a month earlier earned bragging rights for being there before. By the time I arrived, outdated "Lift the Embargo Now" T-shirts were being sold at a steep discount. "Sucker!" Wintle chortled from inside my backpack.

It still felt like an exciting moment in history. The *International Herald Tribune* had been aglow for weeks with reports of banks opening branches in Hanoi and Ho Chi Minh City. Coca-Cola posters were everywhere. Noting a photo of one of the new Vietnam Citibanks, I brought along less cash than usual. I would travel on the cheap and if worse came to worst, I reasoned, "I'll just use an ATM."

Besides, it always feels good to spend less. Some people travel on a budget out of necessity, but others do it for sport. The two inevitably seem to merge, as need becomes a virtue in and of itself; you feel good being cheap even while sleeping on concrete beds and riding third-class makes you feel like crap. Travelers compare their exploits according to how long they've made it and on how little. As anyone who has backpacked knows, he who spends less money is the better person.

This is easier to do if you're a man and can safely conk out anywhere. Wintle could sleep wherever and with whomever he wanted. Not I. One evening, I arrived at the beach resort Nha

Trang with a group of art historians after barreling with them across hundreds of miles of cratered roads to check out some Cham ruins they were into and save myself the bus fare. As soon as the driver stopped the car in town, they trooped off to their comfy hotel, a place that *even took reservations.* "Bye!" they called out, happily anticipating the resort's beachfront amenities.

I, on the other hand, had budgeted ten dollars for my lodgings and had no reservation. It was honeymoon season in Vietnam and every place was full. Somehow, I wound up on the back of a local teenager's motorcycle; he was determined to resolve my situation and I didn't have the luxury of questioning his motive. We crisscrossed the city searching for a place that would let in a single foreign woman; many hotels refused on principle. Finally, he found me lodgings in a roadside cabin I wasn't sure was a hotel at all. The doors to the room closed barn style, and to "lock" them, you had to lift an enormous plank off the floor and drive it through two handles on either side.

Fifteen minutes after I'd changed into pajamas, the plank trembled at a knock on the door. The "helpful" teenager was back to collect his reward. It took a lot of pleading about my husband and small children at home and my honor, and finally, just begging to make him go away. What was I going to do, call the police? Needless to say, there was no phone in the room.

Throughout the entire episode, I felt perversely guilty. Had I led him on? As far as I was concerned, Americans had pretty much fucked Vietnam over for decades, and I was just one more insult to the nation's dignity. Perhaps accepting hotel assistance from a stray teen was a clear sexual advance. In any case, he'd done me a favor and gotten nothing in return, not even a tip.

And, of course, there was Justin Wintle, siding with the

teenager. As often happens with a travel book, the narrator—his opinions, his prejudices, his particular way of viewing things—seeps into your experience. "Serves you right," Wintle said. Maybe I *was* just another clueless American.

By the time I reached Hanoi, then still a car-and-motorcycle-free city where legions of rickety bicycles elegantly wove past one another across massive roundabouts, never colliding, I was out of cash. I'd had to take an impromptu flight from Danang to the north to avoid the bandits then rampant on the overnight train up the coast.

It was time to hit one of those shiny new American bank branches.

There was only one problem. When I finally tracked down the Hanoi Citibank, it was a cubicle in a near-empty office. "Oh no," a solitary clerk said, generously mortified on my behalf. "We're not offering banking services yet. It's just for show right now." He smiled. "Someday!"

I had no money left. I was alone in northern Vietnam. At the kind of establishments I could afford, credit cards were not accepted, and there was no way to pay one off anyway. There was no American Express office. There was no American embassy. In a scene I never would have fathomed my senior year in college, I found myself begging from table to table in a café dominated by European and Israeli tourists, trying not to look like a hippie-dippie backpacking American fool even though I bore all the signs: I was wearing sandals and a pair of faded Thai cotton fisherman's pants. My backpack was grubby, and my hair unwashed. Justin Wintle mocked me as a stupid Yank from inside *Romancing Vietnam*. But Spalding, thank goodness, understood. One day, he assured me, this would be funny.

CHAPTER 11

Wild Swans

Inspirational Reading

Books provoke many reactions (laughter, tears, annoyance, disgust, envy, awe) and stir all kinds of responses (efforts to better oneself, motivation to visit a new city or cook something difficult or vow never to pick up a book by the same author again). But only once did a book get me to starve myself.

It wasn't even a diet book, and I wasn't actually trying to lose weight. But I did go almost entirely without food for four weeks and lost twenty pounds in the process. I felt like I was starving during every moment of every one of those days.

I did it because I was inspired.

This happened in 1994 in China, where I was backpacking solo for six weeks under the aegis of my father, who never would have gone himself. Having watched Bernardo Bertolucci's *The*

Last Emperor at least six times too many, he sent me there in his stead with a thousand-dollar birthday gift earmarked for the trip and instructions to bring him back a spittoon.

A long trip was in the works, but not to China. With the school term in Thailand at an end, and a month spent training at a Thai massage school over, I had hoped to island hop through Indonesia for six weeks. Fellow travelers had scoffed at my first idea of going to India—"You need *at least* six months there, otherwise don't bother." But my father made clear there would be no thousand dollars for either of these countries, much as he loved *The Year of Living Dangerously* and *A Passage to India*. If I wanted the money, it would have to be China—and bring back that spittoon.

I, too, had seen *The Last Emperor*. But I chose as my inspiration a little book called *From Heaven Lake*, by Vikram Seth, the author of the massive novel *A Suitable Boy*. After studying at Nanjing University in the early eighties, Seth had traveled overland across China, through Tibet, and back home to New Delhi and then written a backpacking travelogue about his adventures. It would be fun to follow him, or at least to trace his path along the Chinese portion of the Silk Road. With the bonus from my dad, if I budgeted carefully, I could last six weeks on fifteen dollars a day.

Throughout my year in Thailand, I had discovered the pleasures of reading about the places where you actually were; before living in Asia, I'd tended to read about the faraway— even when I *was* far away, perversely reading about Iowa, for example, while in France. Only now did I realize that if you read about where you were physically, you might get more out of it. I discovered a whole number of travelogues—not only Spalding

Gray's *Swimming to Cambodia*, but also Redmond O'Hanlon's *Into the Heart of Borneo*, Pico Iyer's *Video Night in Kathmandu*, Alexander Frater's *Chasing the Monsoon*—whose authors' daring filled me with awe and determination. I could never do what they'd done (once again my solitary female status counted against me), but I desperately wanted to and I was certainly going to try. This trip to China would be my chance.

It began inauspiciously in Ürümqi. An ethnic Chinese outpost on the Silk Road stretch between Kashgar and Xi'an, Ürümqi is the capital of the western Uighur Autonomous Region, sprawling and industrial and unappealing. The Uighur Autonomous Region is so despised by the Han Chinese, it had served as a place of exile during the more punishing years of Communist rule, and was still populated primarily by Uighurs and Kazakhs, nomadic goatherds of Siberian origin: Muslim, Turkic-language speaking, yurt dwelling. Whenever I looked especially lost in Ürümqi, someone asked if I was Pakistani.

As soon as I disembarked from my first Chinese domestic carrier (not safe, by the way), I realized I'd made a serious miscalculation. Where was the vaporizing heat? *From Heaven Lake*'s opening chapter, "Turfan: July in the Desert," noted, "The only way to remain even tolerably cool in Turfan is to pour cold water on your head and let your hair dry in the air." This, Seth wrote, "happens in minutes and the process can then be repeated."

This was not true, however, in nearby Ürümqi in April, when I arrived from the sweltering summer season of Thailand. Somehow, my brain had processed summer in Thailand as summer everywhere. Though my first moments standing on the austere and gusty tarmac in my cotton fisherman's pants were jarring, I stuck with the plan and booked a tour to the magnificent-sounding

Heaven Lake. Vikram Seth had described it as "an area of such natural beauty that I could live here, content, for a year." According to my guidebook, it was as if a sliver of Canada had been plunked down in the barren depression of the Taksim desert. *It may be slightly cooler there*, I reasoned, donning a windbreaker and tucking an extra pair of socks into a knapsack before stowing the rest of my luggage in a locker.

Heaven Lake certainly seemed like a popular destination. Though there were few tourists at the airport, a throng of guides competed to sign us up for various packages. My little expedition included a Korean football player and a towering former East German border guard. Our guide was a Kazakh dressed in heavy-metal black; he looked about sixteen. The German stared me down and proceeded to interrogate me like a disapproving Stasi officer. "You go on yurt trip as one? Girl alone?"

"Yup, you?" I blinked back. "All by yourself, I take it?" No one in my group really spoke English, but the three others each knew some Mandarin and carried on a stilted conversation among themselves. I wouldn't have minded had there been something else to do. But shortly after we arrived at Heaven Lake, the sky dulled into a desolate gray. The horseback ride component of the vacation package ended early, our numb hands unable to manipulate the reins.

By two o'clock in the afternoon it had grown weirdly dark, especially weird because although it is geographically about four time zones away from Beijing, Ürümqi runs on centralized Beijing time, which meant it was really approximately ten in the morning. The Korean football player squinted at the menacing sky and muttered something in Mandarin; the others nodded solemnly. We lumbered back to the yurt. Feeling betrayed by

Vikram Seth, I switched allegiances and picked up the only other book I'd brought with me, Jung Chang's memoir *Wild Swans: Three Daughters of China*. I sped through the last chapters in the fading light.

Unfortunately, I went too fast and was left with nothing else to read. My other books were in storage back in Ürümqi because I assumed I wouldn't have time to read with all the frolicking at Heaven Lake, which at this point was spiked by piercing cold winds. Now I was trapped in the yurt with no reading material, no one to talk to, and I was hungry. A Kazakh woman cooked our promised meals in a suspect chunk of gray lard, animal origin unknown; sluggish bubbles of fat coagulated in the cauldron of water she used to make tea. No Nescafé for me in the morning, thank you! We were each given a hunk of Kazakh bread that, like a teething biscuit, was malleable enough to be chipped off and swallowed only after a protracted suckle and gnaw.

The others were having fun. The Kazakh rocker whipped out a flask of medicinal-smelling whiskey, and he, the German, and the Korean passed it around, chattering merrily at one another in basic Mandarin, looking askance at me like an intrusive item that had accidentally blown in through the yurt flap. They finally offered some whiskey, but I declined, retreating under a musty pile of ancient blankets. After several hours of repressing my bladder to avoid exploring the outdoor "facilities," I fell asleep, conquered by the ennui.

The next morning, I furrowed my way out from under the six-blanket igloo I'd erected around my shivering form and opened the yurt flap to escape the whiskey-sweat cloud of human bodies and find a hole to pee in. I couldn't believe what I saw, or, rather, didn't see. Outside the yurt was a total whiteout. Several feet of snow had already piled on the ground. We were in the middle of a blizzard.

Panicked, I woke up my hungover yurtmates. The German urged us to ride out the storm, which seemed to work for the football player and the Kazakh rocker, already reaching for the whiskey. The thought of another twenty-four hours in the yurt without food, coffee, water, conversation, or reading material was inconceivable, and I pleaded immediate departure. For a while, it seemed majority would rule, but eventually they cracked. Once I had their reluctant shrugs of assent, I wasted no time pulling on my windbreaker. I shamelessly accepted a flimsy acrylic scarf from the female Kazakh host, who surveyed my unseasonable attire pityingly, and we bolted out into the snow. The roads were impassable.

It was a fourteen-mile hike down the mountain to the nearest village, then another mile through deep Kazakh mud to get to the tour guide's winter house, made of concrete. It turned out the Kazakhs weren't stupid enough to live in mountain yurts during the winter, which in fact extends into June. The solitary yurt we'd stayed in was there only for those tourists fool enough to wander into the desert during low season. No wonder there'd been such competition for Heaven Lake customers.

A vague enmity seemed to have descended on the group, they likely resenting me for the forced trudge. The Korean, the German, the Kazakh, and I barely exchanged words as we stomped our way through the snow. The hike felt endless, though it lasted only a few hours. In the travelogue version of my trip, I would have been appreciating the snowy bluffs and relishing the international company.

Instead, I thought about the book I'd finished in the yurt. The true story of three generations of women suffering through

China's tumultuous twentieth century, *Wild Swans* begins with the author's grandmother, concubine to a Manchurian warlord. Chang's mother was a high official in the Communist Party who was eventually denounced, and Chang herself became a Red Guard during the Cultural Revolution before renouncing communism and moving to London, where she became a professor at the School of Asian Studies. Each of these three women had endured more trauma in any given three-week period than I had in the span of twenty-three coddled American years.

But what really got me was when Jung Chang, along with the rest of China's city youth, roughly 15 million people altogether, was expelled from her school and forced to do hard labor in the countryside because, as Mao put it, "Peasants have dirty hands and cowshit-sodden feet, but they are much cleaner than intellectuals." Even more grueling than the carrying of heavy buckets of water from wells, the husking of grain for food, the aggressive goats guarding the outdoor toilets, was the intellectual deprivation that wore on Chang. "I had an urge to write, and kept on writing with an imaginary pen," she recalled. "While I was spreading manure in the paddy fields . . . I would polish long passages in my mind."

There was no writing; there were no books. "I longed for something to read," Chang recalled. "But apart from the four volumes of *The Selected Works of Mao Zedong*, all I discovered in the house was a dictionary. Everything else had been burned." Per one of Mao's aphorisms, "The more books you read, the more stupid you become." Boredom, Chang discovered, "was as exhausting as backbreaking labor."

Meanwhile, I couldn't even endure the boredom of one bookless, conversation-free evening in a tourist yurt. As I'd lain in the dusty stench the night before, an idea insinuated itself into my head. Chang's tale of woe had greatly moved me, and yet to what end? Could I truly grasp her misery? What did I—could I possibly—know about it? In my Western ease, I'd never experienced the test of real deprivation and the joy of relief. I would never know that kind of emotion firsthand, and that itself felt like a deprivation. How could you become a strong and appreciative person if you'd never had an obstacle to toughen you up?

As grueling as it was, the test of the fourteen-mile trek felt like child's play next to the Chang family's miseries. *Suffer! Suffer, you unappreciative slob,* I scolded myself as I trudged along, as if my rebukes would rid me of a fundamental complacency. *How can you complain about one measly little hike next to the Long March and the Cultural Revolution? Lazy, easy, weak . . . lazy, easy, weak,* I repeated to myself, the winds howling through my flimsy fisherman's pants. *Suffer, suffer.*

By the time we got to the guide's village house and I'd scraped the mud off my canvas sneakers, they were stained crimson with blood. I took off both pairs of what were now deep red-stained socks, and as pain replaced the numbness and my feet swelled before me, I realized my sneakers had been destroyed and my feet along with them. I walked with a crippled gait for days.

But none of this mattered. If anything, it needed to happen. I'd hatched a plan during that trek, something I came to call the Denial Regime. My bloody feet would be an inaugural crusade wound. I photographed my soaked red socks to mark the moment.

The kernel of the Denial Regime had taken shape as I'd watched the Kazakh host cook our lardy, unappealing dinner the night before, knowing I wasn't going to eat a bite of what she made. No matter how hungry, I decided to suffer through it. This got me to thinking. What would happen if you caused yourself to suffer, just to know what it was like?

One of those chronically hungry people who gobbles down candy throughout the day, I have the metabolism and related disposition of a toddler: cranky when unfed. This weakness could be put to use. For the rest of my stay in China, I decided, I would make myself go hungry. Hadn't I moved to Asia in order to challenge myself? Confronting oversize water bugs and a little loneliness didn't necessarily accomplish that.

My self-styled Denial Regime would allow for one small portion of white rice or plain bread a day, a daily vitamin supplement, and a cup of clear soup every few days. I would take it one day at a time, relishing the deprivation, putting off that one portion of starch—*Nope, no eating until at least twelve o'clock. No, make it twelve thirty!*—until I could no longer bear it. I would do this for the rest of my time in China. Others might dread different deprivations, like no showering or no sex, but for me, the prospect of food restriction was the most dreadful. Far worse, I had to admit, than having no books.

If Jung Chang and millions of other Chinese people could live through the horrors of the Cultural Revolution, then certainly it was possible to get through a day without stuffing my face. Every time I felt a pang of hunger, I reprimanded myself, thinking about Jung Chang and repeating my adopted mantra: *Deny, deny.*

It was awful. The hunger never went away for any meaningful amount of time, as in more than ten minutes. Yet the ability to thwart it felt empowering. I felt cleaner, purer, tougher. I've never had an eating disorder, but during those weeks, part of me could disturbingly understand the draw, and the danger. The constant effort only hardened my determination. I felt like a warrior.

The bonus challenge was to make myself focus on the sights I saw during the day and the books I read at night despite the gnawing growls. (Bob bears the marks of this period with a series of easy-to-swallow mass market paperbacks: Michael Crichton's *Congo*, Terry McMillan's *Waiting to Exhale*, Anne Tyler's *Dinner at the Homesick Restaurant*.) Despite these accompanying efforts at self-care, about a week into the Denial Regime, I came down with a sinus infection. Luckily, the sparse language appendix of my outdated Lonely Planet guidebook, which lacked such essentials as "I'm late!" and "Could you *please* keep it down?" included the phrase *wo sher bing* ("I am sick"). It was remarkably effective. No free hotel rooms, you say? *Wo sher bing*, and suddenly a room materialized. The bank teller decides to break for noodles the moment when you walk in? *Wo sher bing* elicited a reluctant compliance.

The effect of *wo sher bing* was so decisive it seemed to carry more weight than just "I'm sick," something more like "I'm pregnant" or "I have cancer." Whatever its implied meaning, *wo sher bing* transformed all my interactions with the Chinese people. One time, I *wo sher bing*'ed a troop of cadres on the train and was forced to ingest copious amounts of unidentified Chinese medicine, inducing a fifteen-hour nap. On another train ride, my sickness persuaded my cabinmates to go to sleep early, allowing me to escape the usual chain-smoking fluorescent banter that pervaded second-class night trains into the wee hours. On yet another ride, a well-dressed man removed a small gadget from his pocket, which he opened, gently tapped, and handed to me.

"Do you need to see a physician?" the screen inquired politely. I leapt on this portable translator with joy, tapping in a detailed response about my symptoms. But the machine had limitations. No matter what message was typed in and no matter what its translation into Chinese, the screen glowed back the same kind query: "Do you need to see a physician?" This, alas, was all the tight-lipped device had to say.

A few people tried to engage me in deeper conversation, to no avail. Not many people spoke English in these small Silk Road towns. Perhaps they were asking for something basic like my destination and when I couldn't respond were as astounded that I didn't speak Mandarin as Americans are when a tourist here doesn't know the rudiments of English. I'd shake my head dumbly until someone would inevitably say with exasperation, "*Ting butong.*" Everyone else seemed to agree this was the case, regarding me sadly and repeating, "*Ting butong.*"

I started to preempt them. Someone would look at me with an expectant air after saying what I imagined was a question and I'd just admit straight out, "*Ting butong.*"

"*Ting butong,*" my conversation partner would confirm, satisfied. "*Ting butong!*" another person would chime in, and they'd lean back and smile ruefully. When I took Mandarin classes years later at NYU I learned a rough translation: "Listens, does not hear." It meant, in short, "She doesn't get it."

Everywhere, I didn't get it. Project Spittoon was a total wash. Don't ask why, but I thought a spittoon was a long tube through which people spat. Thinking back on the many idiotic attempts I made to find one, gesticulating moronically over flutes and similarly shaped items in market after market, makes me blush.

(A spittoon looks, in fact, more like a vase.) "Seriously, Pammy?!" my father groaned when I came back empty-handed.

Backpacking in remote western China in 1994, I was frequently the only tourist in town, and not just the only tourist but also the only white woman by herself and the only white woman by herself wearing inappropriate summer attire and not speaking a word of Chinese, looking sick and tired and hungry as a lost dog. I was obviously some kind of maniac. Every time I sat down constituted a major public event. Staring squads formed. People pointed. Once, as I rested by a public fountain reading, a young man, egged on by onlookers, came forward, reached out, and touched my bare arm before dashing off with a nervous giggle. I stood out in China like a piece from the wrong puzzle.

Watching rickety old men and boxy and bejowled women perform tai chi at the crack of dawn, squat on sidewalks for hours, and pedal profoundly broken bicycles uphill, I felt outdone. I knew that my Denial Regime, demanding though it was, failed to measure up to the physical and psychological challenges the Chinese people had overcome since 1949—and surely well before then, too. But in my own hungry little way, I had to prove that I could endure as well. I spent hours looking forward to my daily bowl of rice, savoring each painstakingly pinched chopstickful, lamenting any wayward grain that plummeted haplessly to the floor. I appreciated every single bite and I appreciated how long I could manage until the next bowl.

The Denial Regime lasted for twenty-eight days, each day recorded in my agenda (Denial 1, Denial 2, Denial 3 ...) like a kind of anti-Bob, listing life's deprivations as Bob chronicled life's gains. The end came two weeks short of my six-week ambition. After a full day exploring the Forbidden City in Beijing, I was assaulted by the godly aroma of hot dan dan noodles topped with fresh cilantro from a stand just outside the city gates. I inhaled the chili and wheaty noodle scent until my brain lit on fire, torching all other thoughts.

"Enough of this madness," I said to myself, abandoning my private revolution. I rushed the noodle stand in a kind of half-wild, semieuphoric state and dove in, barely bothering with chopsticks. It tasted fantastic.

CHAPTER 12

The Secret History

Solitary Reading

Reading for the most part is a solitary downtime activity, yet feels like one that can be done *all* the time, no matter how many people are around. You can will yourself to be alone in a book regardless of circumstance. I for one read when I sit down and I read when I wait and I read while I walk; occasionally I read while I walk into things. I read when I spot a scenic view with a bench (not the point, I know) and to avoid surroundings that are less than appealing. There is something especially enjoyable about reading on trains and on planes and in coffee shops, where the gesture constitutes a futile cultural rebuke to everyone else's tablet or smartphone. They never notice.

But you might not notice things either. You're not necessarily aware of what's going on around you. You miss things and you leave people out, and this might bother others. Some are inherently unnerved by another person reading alone, not seeing it as "I choose to read now," but rather as "Leave me alone" or "I'm lonely." There is something inherently melancholy about reading alone in a restaurant, for example. You get the sad looks that seem to say either "Your date didn't show?" or "You didn't have a date."

And sometimes, if you're me, you can be so oblivious to the signals around you that you end up in trouble. This actually only happened once, but it was decisively unpleasant. I was in Florence. I had just finished a semester abroad in Paris and had a month to spend traveling northward from Rome to the Dolomite mountains. Italy is usually sunny and beautiful, but to the chagrin of the tourist industry and the tourists there that particular month, it rained during every single one of those Italian days. Because youth hostels and convents had no food service, all my meals were eaten out in restaurants and cafés, where I'd arrive alone, pathetic and sopping wet. Each time, I'd steel myself for the host's pitying look when I requested a table for one.

I'd allow these stares to abate before sealing my lowly status by sneaking a book out of my bag. Reading alone at a dinner table in Italy is basically against the law. At the very least, it's culturally insensitive. Apparently, nobody there sees it as a potentially romantic gesture. No one, it seemed, imagined that the solitary reader might secretly hope that if she only read the right book alone, a handsome stranger would come along and ask, "What's that you're reading?" and it would all end happily ever after. Perhaps that was reserved for Audrey Hepburn.

But you could resolve to be open to the possibility—to look up occasionally, to appear friendly, to offer an entrée into conversation, not to be such a New Yorker. This was Italy! These things happened here, at least in fiction.

On my third day in Florence, I was deep into Hemingway's *Nick Adams Stories* (cliché!) over stracciatella at one of the city's premier gelaterias, which I'd carefully selected from my battered copy of *Let's Go*. (My entire budget in Italy went toward food.) As I was waiting for the rain to stop so I could visit a nearby Masaccio fresco, a dapper older gentleman with hat and briefcase approached and asked whether I minded his joining my table. *Be friendly*, I told myself, fighting the instinct to bury nose in book. *He may not be Marcello Mastroianni, but he could be interesting to talk to.* With my tentative assent, the man sat opposite me and then, without word or gesture, a larger man with his own briefcase took the seat next to him and crossed his arms as if he had a train to catch and awaited the precise hour of departure.

The dapper older gentleman spoke fluent English. He spoke fluent French. He spoke knowledgeably about art and literature. He asked about my travels, the details of my itinerary, my background. I was flattered that someone so erudite would bother with my trifling collegiate opinions. Under the spell of his encouragement, I spoke at length. We talked about literature; we talked about art. He knew the Masaccio I wanted to see and was delighted to accompany me there. His driver—he nodded at the man next to him—would take us in his car, parked right outside. Do not worry about the rain.

Just a quick visit to the bathroom first, I explained, watching my manners, keen to impress. On my way back to the table, a man stopped me and whispered urgently, "Run! That man has a gun." I looked up and saw the older gentleman and his thug conferring with each other, maneuvering their briefcases.

And then I ran. The two men got up immediately, pushing their chairs aside, and gave chase. The dapper older gentleman executed a surprisingly nimble leap into a black sedan parked outside; there was already a driver at the wheel, who gunned the engine. The thug bolted after me on foot.

Somehow I managed to lose them, dashing into a church and hiding under a pew. I stayed there for hours, holding my breath. Only when the church filled with a group of tourists did I unfold my body and dart away. Feeling stupid and embarrassed, I didn't go to the police. Instead, I slunk back to my youth hostel, where I confined myself to the vacant girls' dormitory, skipping dinner altogether. What an idiot! What an easy target I'd made. That night, I woke up in a full-sweat panic attack, shaking on the bathroom floor, ready to vomit. Later, I read about Mafia teams kidnapping women to be drugged and sold into sexual slavery abroad; in all likelihood that's what I'd narrowly escaped, if not something "milder" like ransom or rape.

I left Florence first thing the next day. In my haste, I lost my Eurail pass on the train to Lucca. The train ticket had been a graduation gift from my father, and it hadn't been cheap. I certainly didn't have money to buy a new one, and I needed it to last two more months. Feeling rotten, I called him collect from a pay phone to self-flagellate and grovel and beg for another. "I thought you were calling to wish me a happy birthday," he said. "It was yesterday."

I deserved to be alone.

For a long time after that, reading by myself in public made me feel vulnerable. By highlighting my solitude, I'd made myself a mark. *Here I am, come and get me*, I seemed to be signposting to the wolves. I willed myself to become so outwardly tough and impenetrable that nobody would ever again mistake me for someone who was lost. "Go away," my new body language said. "Can't you see I'm reading?"

The worst part was that I loved traveling independently and reading while I did it. Most of the time, I didn't *feel* lost or lonely. Quite the opposite—with a truly engrossing novel, you could feel found. Reading may not always give you full access to the world around you, but it's an entry to *another* world and the company of the people inside it. It's possible to explore two worlds at once.

Books stand out in particularly high relief when you're traveling because during those moments of displacement they also provide a kind of mooring. It's why our memories of what we read when we travel stick with us well after details of the trip itself fade. We remember what we read on the plane, on that beach, in that secluded cabin.

When I look at the characters gathered in my Book of Books from my twenties, my years of solo travel and perpetual singledom, it's hard to feel like I'd ever truly been alone. In France, I'd had Yossarian and Lucie Manette and Becky Sharp and poor Yakov Petrovich Golyadkin. I had my author friends: Gogol and Carrie Fisher and Colette and Arthur Schlesinger and Art Spiegelman. Each place was populated by its own memorable company. In Thailand there were Gabriel Oak and Bathsheba, Bartleby and Ethan Frome and Jeeves; Daniel Boorstin and Martha Gellhorn and Jack London and Edith Wharton; my fellow travelers Ian Buruma, Jan Morris, Patrick Leigh Fermor, and Pico Iyer. And so on with my subsequent travels. They provided companionship.

Browsing through Bob's pages, as I do when trying to recollect a moment, a feeling, an earlier incarnation of myself, I can immediately recall, for example, reading Donna Tartt's *The Secret History* inside the Summer Palace of the Chinese emperor in

Beijing, ignoring everything else around me—the sights, the then intensely blue sky over Beijing before smog overtook the city. My story took place inside my own invented world, one that Donna Tartt started, and that I made complete. This is where I really was. When I think back to that afternoon, what I remember is less the gold and red and blue painted bridges and the ornate gardens that surrounded me and more the rush of excitement that I felt as I accompanied Tartt's scheming coterie of murderous college students. I carried the book with me everywhere I went in Beijing and into bed at night, following Tartt's characters. I knew exactly where I was and I didn't feel alone at all.

CHAPTER 13

The Wisdom of the Body

In Love with a Book

Sometimes you fall so much in love with a book that you simply have to tell everyone, to spread the love and to explain the state you're in. You read passages aloud to anyone who will listen. You wait with bated breath, watching for signs of appreciation, wanting that smile, that laugh, that nod of recognition. Please love this book too, you silently—and sometimes not so silently—urge. You become insistent, even messianic in your enthusiasm.

And sometimes you fall in love with a person, and you're pretty much the same way. Everyone needs to know about him and appreciate him and admire him—and you for being the one to have found him. You need the love to radiate in every possible direction. That person, more than all other people, must appreciate you and all your attendant objects of love, your stories, your authors, your characters, just as you appreciate him. So he can know you and understand you. You want to enter his secret world, and let him into yours.

To allow someone into my Book of Books would be a true test of intimacy, and trust. There, in those pages, after all, were my fleeting passions and yearnings, my literary crushes, my love life on the page. Some of it demanded explanation. Without annotation, there was no demarking the books I'd hated from the ones I'd admired, books I'd misunderstood, books I'd disliked intensely. All of it was just laid out there, at once revealing and yet open to misinterpretation. Someone would have to really know me to understand.

Though I'd never shown him to anyone, I'd told a few people about Bob in the past. This turned out to be a dicey proposition. Not everyone loved my Book of Books. "Tallying up books like the ticking off of accomplishments," one boyfriend said accusingly, as if I'd admitted to quantifying parental love or indexing my inner beauty. "Hurry up, go note it in Bob," he'd gibe every time I closed a book, as if the act of recording invalidated the entire experience. Were the books truly being read for their own sake or in pursuit of some goal that sullied the entire enterprise?

"What does this tell you if you don't remember anything about the books themselves?" another beau asked, suggesting an expanded Bob with a page for my impressions of each book in its stead. This Bigger Bob lasted for two books, the relationship not much longer. "You're not seriously going to allow books on tape, are you?" wondered a third, scornfully. Competition, jealousy, misunderstandings, risk. Perhaps it wasn't worth the bother.

It wasn't until my midtwenties, when I'd met the person I would marry, that I truly opened Bob up to someone else. I had never been one of the girls who'd always had a boyfriend; the right guys always seemed to be with someone else. I ended up with the wrong guys, the ones who didn't get me or whom I didn't get, and we usually broke up hastily as a consequence.

This guy was different. There was nothing to prove to him; he loved me for who I was. He loved me no matter what. And I knew he would love Bob, too. There was no way he would be put off by my Book of Books because he was unquestionably much better read; moreover, he actually remembered what he read. Here was someone who had actually finished his Plato and Hobbes and Locke; for him, the *Norton Anthology* was a footnote. Marrying him would be like uploading an entirely new database to my brain.

When we met, I was reading Sherwin Nuland's surgeon's-eye view of human biology, *The Wisdom of the Body*. Bodies were on my mind because at that time, by some terrible misunderstanding, I'd been put to work on the *Sports Illustrated* swimsuit calendar—without doubt, a professional nadir.

I was twenty-six, living in Brooklyn, and had just started working at Time Inc. with great expectation, leaping from the child's playpen of Scholastic Inc.'s downtown headquarters, where I'd worked for three years, to the big-boys' club in the midtown Time-Life Building. After all my angsting over what to do with my life, I'd wound up moving back from Thailand to New York, abandoning a plan to switch over to Hong Kong, and taking a half-editorial, half-marketing job in publishing when it materialized during a pre-Internet visit to my old stomping ground, the college alumni services office. Miraculously, this job paid well enough that I could afford to live with just one roommate in the East Village, which was possible back when you could rent a room in Manhattan for four hundred dollars a month.

Bob returned to New York with me, and his pages began to fill with stories signifying that I was Home. Robert Caro's *The Power Broker*, Theodore Dreiser's *Sister Carrie*, Stephen Crane's *Maggie: A Girl of the Streets* (my penchant for dark reading alive and brooding), H. L. Mencken's *My Life as Author and Editor*, *Money* by Martin Amis, and Dorothy Parker's short story "Big Blonde" helped inform the kind of urban life I wanted to live and the kind I hoped to avoid. ("Please let me never be Big Blonde," was one recurring thought.) Asia could still be visited in books, but I was living in New York City, no longer a mecca but mine, and I wanted to be fully there.

The publishing division I signed up for at Time Inc. was charged with creating books based on the company's venerable quarry of magazines. I envisioned myself assembling handsome pictorial histories of World War II from the pages of *Time*, sifting dreamily through the photographic archives of *Life* and writing elegant and elegiac captions for each entry in the sumptuous coffee table books I'd help produce.

What actually happened was that I, the least sportif person within a twelve-block radius of the Time-Life Building, was assigned to work on *Sports Illustrated*. Not only that, I was put on the swimsuit calendar. It wasn't even a book.

My team consisted of three people. Jack, my boss, was blond, chipper, blue-suited, and sporty, the most all-American person I'd ever met. One of the photo editors we worked with was a European named Guillermo and every time Jack gamely addressed him, it came out differently: "Gwermo." "Gallermo." "Germo." Charlotte, the third person on the team, was unnervingly efficient; she had a system and color-coded pattern for everything. I struggled to ape her every move. "Wait, what are the purple thumbtacks

for?" "Do you use the five-by-seven index cards for the B48 mail-
ing, or the four-by-six?" (Later, I learned that she sorted Tupper-
ware as a stress-reducing activity—try it!) The rest of my work
there was not nearly as inspiring.

Luckily, I'd found a new source of inspiration. I met him
through a graphic designer who'd worked on publications we'd
each been editing, across town, in different offices. ("He talks so
lovingly about his mother!" she enthused.) It was my first ever
head-over-heels, totally irrational, and irresponsible relationship.
The moment he proposed, I accepted with an immediate and
giddy yes. He lived on the Upper West Side and I lived in Carroll
Gardens, I had two cats and he was violently allergic, he was
about to move to London for grad school and I had a brand-new
job in New York—but the how and the when of the happily-ever-
after was mere detail. For the first time in my life, I didn't care
how everything would be arranged. It just would.

In that moment, both heady and earthy at once, it felt right
to be reading a book called *The Wisdom of the Body*, an appropriate subject for the early days of a relationship. Sherwin Nuland's
follow-up to his bestselling *How We Die* toured the reader through
the human body from the nervous system to the digestive system
and, of course, the heart. Everything seemed to point to the same
place. Citing Shelley's "A Defence of Poetry," Nuland wrote,
"Without imagination of another's mind there can be no understanding of that other and therefore no love." He was talking
about us. Everything was about us. I was in thrall to my own
heart, reason be damned.

Weirdly, the part of the book I most remember sharing in
this besotted state was a harrowing passage about a third-place
beauty pageant winner who'd eaten too much pork and had an

unlikely adverse reaction. "She was throwing herself around the gurney and shouting for help—evidently not fully conscious . . ." And later, "The pattern of blotch and pallor involved every visible inch of body and was much deeper in its purplishness than I had ever encountered, except on the freshly dead." I read it to my fiancé as we lay on a futon on the floor of his apartment, and we both shrieked in horror and fascination. He got everything.

The second he asked me to go with him to London, abandoning my cats to the mercy of a stranger and giving up my two-bedroom Brooklyn floor-through with working fireplace for only a thousand dollars a month and blowing my nascent publishing career out the window, I said, "Let's go!" One lesson I'd gleaned from living in Thailand was that everything would be there when I got back. And until then, who cared? There was only time with him and the time until I would next be with him; I could hardly see where I was going.

Just a week before, my colleague Charlotte had given notice too. Her husband, a banker, was being relocated to London. With both of us leaving him in the lurch in the span of a month to cross the Atlantic, Jack looked like he didn't know what hit him.

So what? I was in love! Other people's suffering was of no consequence; everything would surely make its way to a happy ending. Within weeks I was living in Tony Blair's New Britannia, spending my days walking and biking around the city, sitting on park benches reading English literature and eating curry takeaway. We Chunneled to Paris for a weekend so I could show him off to the Mathieus for their approval. "*Très beau,*" Carole and Bertrand agreed. "But you need to do something about his French." At night, he and I lay in bed reading *Down and Out in Paris and London*, first he, then I, then both of us reading sections aloud to each other, laughing, grimacing, commiserating, fans of everything Orwell and seemingly everything else, perfectly in sync.

At night, we curled up on the sofa in our little duplex in Fulham (London being far more affordable then), just across the bridge from Putney, which would later figure so vividly in Hilary Mantel's novel *Wolf Hall*. We'd turn off the overhead, light a few candles, and play audiobooks—*Heart of Darkness* and *The Hobbit*—on a small portable stereo, pretending we were in an earlier radio age, listening to serialized stories in the dark. He didn't object to audiobooks being entered in Bob.

We loved stories about the perfidy of man and gusty adventures at sea. Melville and Conrad were our cornerstones: *Billy Budd, Sailor* and the sinister treachery and vengeance of *Benito Cereno*. We took turns reading *Lord Jim*. I told him about my favorite Conrad story, "The Secret Sharer," and my dream of one day writing a screenplay adaptation, and he took me seriously. He introduced me to *Darkness at Noon*, and on his recommendation I read *Angle of Repose*, and we bonded over the cold, enclosed prisons of Stalin's gulag and the hard, spare plains of Wallace Stegner's American West.

Together, we took trips to Wales and York and Scotland, listening to books in the car, attuned to the literature of our destination: Robert Louis Stevenson's *Kidnapped* and Elizabeth George's *Payment in Blood* as we waited for goats to pass across the narrow streets on the Isle of Skye. On vacation in the States, we listened to adventure stories en route to Nantucket: *Into Thin Air* and *Into the Wild* and *The Perfect Storm*. Like me, he was an enthusiast, and when we discovered something new we seized on it together, almost gasping with pleasure over dramatic scenes. Whenever one of us introduced an old favorite, we savored the other's first delight like a shared meal eaten with a newly acquired gusto, as if we'd never truly tasted it before.

There was only one literary challenge left to overcome: poetry, which he of course appreciated instinctively, and memorized with ease. It was time. I needed to as well because we needed to find a poem. Every couple, after all, recited one at their wedding. It was basically a matrimonial requirement, like a purification ritual in the face of nuptial excess. And lo, miraculously and yet as if foreordained, we found our poem.

On a perfectly sun-dappled September afternoon, in front of friends and family in a flower-strewn copse in upstate New York, I hardly noticed anyone else was there as he read to me Rainer Maria Rilke's "Love Song":

> How shall I hold on to my soul, so that
> it does not touch yours? How shall I lift
> it gently up over you on to other things?
> I would so very much like to tuck it away
> among long lost objects in the dark
> in some quiet unknown place, somewhere
> which remains motionless when your depths resound.
> And yet everything which touches us, you and me,
> takes us together like a single bow,
> drawing out from two strings but one voice.
> On which instrument are we strung?
> And which violinist holds us in the hand?
> O sweetest of songs.

I loved and even understood the poem.

CHAPTER 14

The Magic Mountain

Different Interpretations

It turned out the relationship wasn't all mutual appreciation and understanding. Our fight over *The Magic Mountain* was prolonged and bitter and, in all likelihood, entirely in my head. Nevertheless, my husband had started it.

He was the one who had introduced me to Thomas Mann. I'd read his copy of *Buddenbrooks* in a swoon, and we immediately decided to take turns with *The Magic Mountain*, considered by many to be Mann's masterpiece. That much we agreed on. Yet somehow, every time we talked about what was in the novel itself, things got testy. *The Magic Mountain*, with its complex geopolitics and layers of meaning, struck a discord.

Mann originally wrote *The Magic Mountain* after visiting his wife in a swanky sanatorium in Davos, Switzerland, where she was trying to recover her health. In the novel, Mann's protagonist, Hans Castorp, in his early twenties and about to embark on a career in shipbuilding, similarly travels to Davos, but to visit his cousin; he ends up staying on for years. There were certain eerie parallels at work. My husband and I had recently decamped to Europe. We, too, were isolated from our friends at home. We, too, weren't quite sure what we were doing there.

Worse, we soon turned against each other. *The Magic Mountain* is by most accounts a deliberately ambiguous book, part satire, part social critique, part prophetic history. A good chunk of the novel is taken up by philosophical debates between two characters, Settembrini and Naphtha, curdled by the snide insinuations they volley back and forth. Naphtha: " 'What Herr Settembrini neglects to add is that the Rousseauian idyll is merely a rationalist's bastardization of the Church's doctrine...' " And from Settembrini: " 'Even war, my dear sir, has on occasion been forced to serve progress—as you yourself must grant me...' "

Somehow their endless quarrels became our own. We argued over who Settembrini and Naphtha were and what they were meant to symbolize and what they were arguing about. We could agree on nothing other than that we disagreed with everything the other person said. All the while, I wondered whether we were really arguing about Settembrini and Naphtha, or whether we were stand-ins for these characters—and if so, which one was I? The secular humanist Lodovico Settembrini, I'd like to have thought, even though he is considered by many to be a caricature of Weimar-era liberalism. Then again, I couldn't be his adversary Leo Naphtha either, and anyone insinuating as much could just fuck off. Naphtha was a radical and a Marxist, and I despised the things he stood for. But then, who the hell was supposed to be Naphtha? We couldn't both be Settembrini.

It didn't matter. We'd ended up on opposite sides of the book, and this was only the bad beginning. Why were we even fighting about these imagined people? Why were we fighting at all? We had only just run off to London to embark on the rest of our lives. It couldn't possibly have gone wrong already.

Obviously, two people in a relationship can't always love the same things or understand why someone loves something you hate or reads it in a different way. We all know this, even if we don't always entirely believe or abide by it, especially if we're twenty-six and fully persuaded that true love means that disagreements are meaningless. Or that where there is True Love, disagreements naturally evolve into something adorable, to be laughed over in rom-com montage with a tender embrace and exhilarating makeup sex at the end. Or that two people in love must love everything about the other, even the things one person hates.

But it became clear that the minute a subject veered from the fictional world, the private world, the secluded, just-us-on-top-of-the-mountain world, into the greater, grittier territory below, the nonfictional world, my husband and I had serious differences. Even when we each happily read those same books about the perfidy of man, we read them in opposite ways. For me, a book like *The Magic Mountain* contested my essentially optimistic take on the world rather than overturned it; by forcing me to reexamine my convictions, it strengthened and reaffirmed them. Whereas for him, the world really *was* that bleak, and books proved it.

I found that I liked to read books that challenged my point of view; he seemed to prefer to read books that confirmed his. He probably thought the same thing of me, only the opposite. In an essay called "Why Readers Disagree," the critic Tim Parks theorizes that two people may see the same book differently in much the way misunderstandings occur within newly formed couples, because "people have grown up with quite different criteria for assessing behavior and establishing a position in relation to it." It was as if our fundamental differences became manifest in how we read, slicing through the fog of infatuation. Who were we, and how exactly had we ended up together, the words on the page seemed to be asking.

None of this was really about the books. But under the circumstances, it was hard to enjoy what I was reading anymore, at least not in the same way. Already I was changing. My Book of Books had begun to reflect my husband's interests, deliberately so. I wanted to know what he knew. I wanted our minds to align in a way that reflected our hearts. His books would be mine, too, part of our shared life. That's not entirely what happened.

Nonfiction, where our disagreements were more starkly exposed, was even worse than fiction. Any book could set us at odds, and did. Read *Modern Times*, the defining road map to the twentieth century, my husband urged me; *then* I would understand his worldview. I'd had some previous Paul Johnson experience, having been suckered into the History Book-of-the-Month Club in high school the way normal kids signed up for Columbia House Records. Johnson's *Intellectuals* was part of my ninety-nine-cent first shipment. Completely unaware of his politics, I'd read each essay in a state of growing confusion. Why was Johnson taking down each of these venerated philosophers? What did he have against Rousseau?

Still, I ventured into my husband's *Modern Times* blushingly naïve. I didn't know about Johnson's slavish Thatcherism, his ardent defense of Nixon, his admiration for Pinochet, or the way he overtly manipulated historical fact to suit his political disposition. Here, I assumed, would be a useful brush-up on twentieth-century Europe.

Now that I was reading Johnson as a somewhat older, more sophisticated reader, one who'd actually studied European history in college (maybe having learned something after all), it came through quite clearly on the page. How was it possible my husband liked this guy? Johnson, I worried, was telling me something I didn't want to know about the man I was in love with. Was it possible I didn't know him at all?

That's when I started reading behind his back. And Bob began to tell a different story, one populated by books that made an alternate case. These were books my husband had no interest in, books that perhaps opposed his interests. One day, browsing in Hatchards in Piccadilly Circus (the best London bookstore, btw), I came upon an essay in a Christopher Hitchens collection in which Hitchens described with gleeful and damning detail Johnson's drunken boorishness and general despicability. Hitchens recalled watching Johnson bully a female foreign editor at the *New Statesman*. Here's Hitchens's description of Johnson:

> "Don't listen to her, she's a Communist!" he kept bellowing, his face twisted and puce with drink. "Fascist bitch!" he finally managed, before retiring to a sofa on the other side of the room and farting his way through a fitful doze for the rest of the meal.

Hitchens had proved my case: Johnson was no authority. Read *Modern Times*, my husband had urged me; *then* I would understand. Now I feared I understood too much.

In any case, all this sleuthing was for naught. One of the worst aspects of arguing with my husband was that he unfailingly emerged victorious. Whereas my own memory was a dismal chamber of half-forgotten, half-thought-out notions that leaked precipitously, my husband's was well stocked and airtight. Nothing fell out. He knew everything, or at least everything that proved him right. Mention Poland, and he could describe the country's nineteenth-century history in detail; bring up Kentucky, and he had the name of every senator who had represented the state at the ready. Every single word he read he absorbed, digested with a cogent point of view, formulated into persuasive arguments, and then filed where it could be accessed at a moment's notice, and, it seemed, used against me.

This remarkable retention initially filled me with awed admiration. Here was someone I could learn from, like having my own private library of a husband. "Click on him!" was a running joke among his friends when one of them had trouble remembering a fact or date. And now here he was, by my side, entirely clickable. But over time, my enthused approval congealed into an unattractive envy and, later still, a rage at him and a loathing for myself. How unfair that I didn't share this skill, and what an asshole he could be when he used it so effectively against me.

It was just the two of us. We had few friends in London. Exceedingly efficient Charlotte had arrived from Time Inc. only a few weeks before me, and was already pregnant and working at Condé Nast; she and her husband lived perfectly in Chelsea with a ready-set crowd of professional expats who hosted well-orchestrated dinner parties. My husband's new friends were a ragtag group of twenty-two-year-old grad students who wanted to talk about what they needed to study that night. I felt out of place in both worlds, neither student nor employee.

Unfortunately, there wasn't an easy way to meet other people. Without official working papers, finding a full-time position at an actual company was a legal impossibility. The only loophole for an American was to prove that no one else in the European Union could do the job. With only a few years' media experience under my belt, I could hardly pretend. Would-be employers at various Time Warner affiliates shrugged their shoulders helplessly.

Outside of job interviews, everyone assumed I was a housewife. Utility workers unfailingly addressed me as Missus and they weren't far off the mark. Much of my day was spent food shopping, gym going, and household tending. My husband had a little money, so I could afford not to work. Don't worry about it, he reassured me; after all, I was the one who'd had to quit a job to move to London. Having worked since I was fourteen and risen to the dubious title of "marketing manager" (yet another reason to ditch the Time Inc. job), I felt gratitude, guilt, discomfort, defensiveness, relief, fear, anxiety, and a growing sense of indolence. I roasted lamb chops.

On the bright side and for the first time in my life, I managed to land actual freelance work as a writer and editor, and was even paid small amounts of money for the privilege. After meeting a couple of editors at the *Economist* and sweating through a tryout, I was given a small monthly column on global arts trends. I could hardly believe my good fortune. Slightly less luckily but far more lucratively, I started editing internal publications for McKinsey, the global consulting firm and a place where nearly everyone wrote in jargon using English as a second language.

Both jobs taught me a lot about the work that went into good writing, building an argument, backing it up, and making a point. The first not only required me to write well, it also asked that I do so in a British accent; the second involved making bad writing less bad. But neither job, largely conducted from our London flat, did much to alleviate my feelings of isolation. On those occasions when I went into the *Economist*'s St. James headquarters, the plummy tones of the extremely English people who worked there scared me into near silence. For the first time in my life I was living with a partner, and I'd never felt more alone.

Here we were, having practically just met and now living together in London, separated from friends, family, jobs, and—not unlike Hans Castorp—cast away from our larger social tapestry. In theory and occasional reality, this was a lovely way to be in love. But with few other outlets, we began to turn against each other. We disagreed about books, we disagreed about politics, we had different worldviews, and we disagreed about the way each of us characterized the other. We were still in love; we just found each other disagreeable.

With growing frequency, the world out there became the basis for argument. I started to read with an eye to anticipating the fights; I'd lap up books, magazines, and newspapers with purpose, accumulating statistical backup and rebuttals for future intellectual showdowns. "Aha!" I'd gloat, when I found a particularly useful piece of data in an article or book, scribbling notes that I'd file away for future reference.

I was still no match for him. He could pull out a quote by Kant that he'd barely glanced at during a freshman-year seminar and swashbucklingly apply it to something I'd said, rendering it stupid and inert.

And he knew it. A year later, lying in our bed in Brooklyn, where we'd moved after London, he playfully pinned me down in bed and demanded to know the hero's name from Somerset

Maugham's *Of Human Bondage*. I'd finished reading the novel only six months before. "His object of desire's name was Mildred," I answered miserably. Though I'd spent more than six hundred pages with the character, I couldn't for the life of me remember his name. (It's Philip.)

This put me constantly on my guard. My defensiveness had the unintended consequence (a favorite phrase of his) of making me a better reader, a closer reader, cautious and more skeptical. In earlier blithe days, I'd simply allowed the content of books to gather agreeably in my head as I read and then file out when I was done. Now I clung to texts with determination, stowing away facts for future reference. I needed to be prepared.

If my childhood had made me an ambitious and voracious reader and my high school English teacher had turned me into a close reader, my husband made me a deeper reader and a more critical one. I'd gone from escaping into books and searching for answers to locating a considered remove, respecting my perspective on the work, and trusting my own responses. I hadn't properly engaged with books before I'd met my husband; I'd never wrestled with a text. Before we were married, I'd never written a book review; a few months after we split up, I wrote my first.

And a funny thing happened when I devoted myself to the authors I vehemently disagreed with: I found I enjoyed reading them. There's a personal and intellectual challenge in being forced to inhabit another point of view, to reexamine your opinions and learn to make a case for them. As all debaters know, sometimes you figure out what you really think only when in opposition. If reading people who think along the same lines as you do is a comfort, reading the people with whom you disagree is discomfiting—in a good way. It's invigorating. To actively grapple with your assumptions and defend your conclusions gives you a sense of purpose. You come to know where you stand. Even if that means standing apart.

Later, when it was all over, after the wedding and the separation and the divorce, it was hard to prevent the arguments from continuing to swirl around in my head. I couldn't stop reading defensively, endlessly poised to prove that there was more than one side to any story.

I missed it. But what to do with that yearning for engagement? My husband was gone, living on another continent, and I was still putting up a fight. The positioning, the ready indignation, the fear of not having the facts marshaled by my side continued to wind up my brain as I scoured the newspaper over coffee and as I read any book, fiction or nonfiction, Victorian novel or twentieth-century biography. I'm ready now, I thought to myself. I know who I am. But the person I wanted to appreciate all that was no longer there.

For months and even years after we split, years in which we never actually spoke, I'd pull my ex into conversations about what I was reading, whether it was Steven Pinker's *The Language Instinct* or Dean Acheson's *Present at the Creation* or Howard Zinn's *A People's History of the United States*, which I expected he would think I liked because he'd always seemed to reduce me to simplistic views. It had felt unfair then, and it still stung. Well, I'd show him. I paused midbook and conjured him in my mind.

"You didn't think I'd agree with you on this one, did you?" I asked, relishing what I knew would be surprise and a glimmer of respect. I'd play and push repeat on endless variations of our ensuing discussion. We would debate back and forth over books we disagreed on and issues that had torn us apart. Only now we no longer quarreled so much; our views had mellowed. The rare times we fought, I won.

CHAPTER 15

Autobiography of a Face

On Self-Help

Is there any genre as potentially embarrassing as self-help? Diet books, parenting guides, sex manuals, relationship fix-its; these are the books that hide beneath the *New Yorker* or within a bathroom magazine rack. Some people consider themselves above the very idea. They disdain any overt effort at self-improvement or consider how-to's ludicrous. Others, and they have a point, think *all* books are a form of self-improvement.

For me, the best self-help has always been reading about other people's problems. From an early age, I lapped up accounts of mental illness and abuse (*The Three Faces of Eve*, *Sybil*, *I Never Promised You a Rose Garden*, *One Child*), other people's suffering providing my own guilty salve. Reading about other people feeling bad can make you feel a little bad and eventually come around to making you feel good, or at least better. Whatever they're dealing with always seems legitimately far worse than what one is going through, or at least much more interesting. And it's an easy way to avoid one's own problems.

That may explain why, in the summer of 1999 and in the death throes of my marriage, I decided to read a book about other people's bad marriages. I brought it along as ballast when my husband and I traveled to Texas to witness two of my perfectly happy friends getting perfectly married. The book was *Group* by Paul Solotaroff, a field guide to the life-lived-less-than-well. Solotaroff had done a kind of gonzo reporting in the psychotherapy world, sitting in on a year of group therapy with the understanding that he would write about it at the end. The result was a riveting account of troubled sex lives, entrenched personal foibles, and pending divorces. It was a book about therapy to be read as therapy.

Shortly after we returned from Texas, three weeks shy of our first anniversary and two days after our wedding pictures finally arrived from the photographer, my husband and I got divorced. I should say we decided to get divorced; in New York at that time, you had to wait a year to finalize the state's version of a "no-fault" divorce on the charmless grounds of "abandonment." The morning before Labor Day weekend, my husband initiated what I could not, stuck as I was in the story line of ever after, no matter how unhappily. Within weeks, we'd cut off all communication and put an ocean between us.

Divorce is hard enough when you know that you're done with a marriage; when you still feel like you're in the middle of one, it is gut splitting. It was as if my entire existence had rested on a magic carpet rather than a concrete foundation, and it was ripped out from under me. As a married person, I had banked on the idea, however illusory, that I knew the beginning, middle, and end of my—of our—story. If I wasn't married, then I wasn't part of the narrative that had gripped me so fully and wholeheartedly from the moment we'd gotten engaged. It knocked the wind out of me. I couldn't breathe.

When I was nine and packing a suitcase with one of my brothers on the second floor of an A-frame rental in the Catskills, the suitcase shifted, sending me careening backward over a balcony, twelve feet down to the hardwood floor below. I still have a mental image of my feet overhead, hair obstructing my view, and then a *whump* as I landed and reverberated back up like a ball momentarily drawn by the suction of a vacuum cleaner, the air forced out of my lungs, before I slumped back to the ground and went into shock.

"T-t-tt-t-t-t-t-tt-t-t-t-tt-t," I jabbered mechanically for a long minute (this part I don't remember) while my brothers giggled nervously. As soon as I regained consciousness, everyone was herded into the car home. I was given the front seat for the first time, rather than the Way Back, where I'd usually hang my head in misery under a cloud of stale Salem smoke and car exhaust. But I couldn't even appreciate this first-class status; I leaned my stinging head against the window, consumed with shame. I had fallen like an idiot in front of everyone, made a ridiculous noise, and now we had to leave early, ruining the weekend for everybody. A bowl rested in my lap in case I threw up, an urge I suppressed with all my might, determined not to make things worse.

This was exactly how I felt now. Once again, I had failed spectacularly for all to see. I'd summoned my family members, all my friends—the Mathieus had flown in from France, for goodness sake—everyone I knew and loved and wanted to think well of me to my wedding barely a year earlier, and now I'd ruined it, wasting everyone's time and money, and losing their respect in the process. Everyone had been let down.

I had always known that one day I was going to get in trouble and now I had; the only benefit I could think of—and I didn't think of it until later, when I'd recovered enough to start thinking again—was that I would never let it happen again. Not that I wouldn't get in trouble again; I knew I would. But I would never let myself be caught so off guard. The mistake had been thinking I was somehow above fucking up royally, that I was safe. But I had been just as vulnerable and oblivious as anyone else, and reading all the books in the world couldn't have saved me.

And I was pretty sure nobody would let me forget it. It's terrible to feel cast out of the smug married club, the group that could show up at the ten-year college reunion with all their boxes ticked off, cheerful toddlers scampering underfoot. Now I would be a blight, a cautionary tale. There might not be any other divorcées there. Everything that married people knew—whom they lived with, what their plans were next weekend and next year, what they wanted out of life—I suddenly didn't know anymore. The baby names we'd picked out, for naught. My two former cats, living with a stranger. Our plans to retire in Bali. The stories we'd share with our grandchildren. My entire sense of the long-term was gone.

The day-to-day was no easier. The first instinct was to call my ex-husband for comfort, to tell him how hard it was to get from morning to night and then through those long nighttime hours. But on whom do you unload your pain when the person you unload it on is no longer there and, worse, is the person who inflicted it? Talking to other people wasn't much easier. "I had no idea!" was the common response. Or: "You never know what goes on in a marriage." Even when it's your own.

Whatever other people said to me, no matter their intention, felt less a consolation and more like judgment. Not only was my ex being judged, but the wisdom of the marriage itself, the quality of the person going into it and staying there, the implications, me. If he was so awful, why did I marry him? If there were such problems, how could I not have known? What the hell was wrong with me? The author of a bad story, one with a no-good, fool heroine and an ugly ending.

And it was hard to get out. The marriage didn't last long, but I hadn't known that would be the case when it began. Everything had been planned with an eye to forever. In the early, heady days of romance, I'd given my husband unprecedented access to Bob. He'd loved my Book of Books so much he'd asked if it could be his as well. I'd let him fill his own completed books into Bob's pages, starting from the back and working forward, toward mine, becoming part of my diary and as much a part of me as anyone ever had. At some point, perhaps in our dotage, we imagined our two book lists would meet at Bob's center.

When we split up, I ripped out those pages and gave them back. (He asked.) I'd been so careful, so self-protective, for so long. I should never have let someone else write in my Book of Books. I swore never to break Bob again. For now, I put him aside, the damaged record too painful to revisit.

Because the marriage ended inconveniently on a three-day weekend, a shift in plans was required; the scheduled visit to the in-laws clearly no longer in the cards. Somehow, my weepy body was relocated upstate to my father's house in Woodstock.

Was it the second night after my husband put an end to things? The third? There was one night in Brooklyn, wailing in despair, inconsolable; the rest was a blur.

Upstate, one of my brothers and his girlfriend drove me to a mall where they installed me at the movie *In Providence*; I think it was supposed to be a comedy. I stared at the screen, sobbing. At that moment every story was a tragedy.

Too mired in my own sorrows to get interested in anyone else's, for the first time I was unable to read. Bob lay forlornly, untouched, on a shelf; I had no desire to reflect or reminisce. There was nothing good to be found in it. Every book I opened, no matter how comedic or superficial, came back to me and my failure. There was no escape reading. The morning headlines, Enid Nemy's "Metropolitan Diary" in the *Times*, a breezy *Vanity Fair* article about a long-forgotten Las Vegas scandal, it didn't matter what—in a miracle of thematic unity, everything managed to be about my heartbreak, every story thread getting tangled in the shreds of my unraveling life. People say that divorce is like a death and, insofar as I felt like part of me had died along with my marriage, they were right.

The week after we split, my ex and I met in our forsaken apartment to divvy up belongings, parceling out furniture and taking turns claiming the antiques we'd splurged on during our honeymoon in Bali and Chiang Mai only eleven months earlier. We hadn't been together long, but we'd accumulated a lot—the year in London, the visits to France, six weeks in Greece and Turkey; there were carpets.

Hardest to parse were the books. It was easy enough to distinguish his monumental hardcover tomes from my used college paperbacks. We knew which books had come from his personal library or mine. But what of the books we'd acquired together? Mutual dreams were bound together in so many of those pages.

"You can have *Joseph and His Brothers*," I offered. We'd both planned to be Thomas Mann completists and had gotten an especially attractive early edition to share.

"Thank you," he said. I'm not sure he realized that with that I was giving him Us. We had plotted wanting to read it together and he had given it to me as a gift. In returning it, I was saying farewell to any together plans.

Somehow I got us out of our Brooklyn lease, left the starter apartment that had overnight become a morgue, and moved to a sad divorcée's one-bedroom next to the Morgan Library. Though not properly a public library, it felt close enough. A start on a new page.

I was finally forced back into reading when, in one of life's great ironic twists, I was asked to write my very first book review, and the book was Susan Faludi's *Stiffed: The Betrayal of the American Man*. I almost felt ready to write it. At the moment I was feeling very much betrayed by the American man.

"Oh, dear," my editor said when I handed my piece in. "Let me show you how to write a book review." I did have one nice turn of phrase, which he kindly kept.

Meanwhile, a new books editor had joined the *Economist*, and when I tearfully explained that I might need an extra week to finish my monthly column, she got me on a plane to London, put me up in a hotel on the Thames, and asked me to work on an editorial project involving the magazine's cultural coverage. I was back in a city that had been ours, but it wasn't the same place it had been just a year before. I steered clear of our old neighborhood, trying to sear a new imprint on the city so it wouldn't become a place defined by past disappointment. I didn't want to lose London. This would become a pattern—getting back up on the bike and revisiting the places he and I had been to, trying to reclaim them. He couldn't have London, or Paris, or Amsterdam. These were the settings of *my* story too.

When I finally found my way back to leisure reading, it was to read the dark, sad memoirs of darker, sadder people, any heartbreak more worthy than my own. I read Calvin Trillin's *Remembering Denny*, his affecting tribute to a college classmate who had committed suicide. I read Jean-Dominique Bauby's *The Diving Bell and the Butterfly*, which the former editor of French *Elle* dictated using a single blinking eye after a car accident left him with locked-in syndrome, unable to move or communicate in any other way. Misery memoirs made good company.

In my wallowing, I leaned on other people's resilience. I read *Days of Obligation: An Argument with My Mexican Father* by Richard Rodriguez. I read the transgender travel writer Jan Morris's second memoir, *Pleasures of a Tangled Life*. I read *Lost in Translation: Life in a New Language* by Eva Hoffman. I envied other people's hardiness.

But no matter how hard I tried to dive into other people's stories, it felt impossible not to get mired in my own, which rattled in my head like a taunting earworm. No matter how many times I tearfully recounted my unhappiness to friends, trying to get it out, it stayed on, preoccupying by day and haunting by night. Maybe I could somehow write it out of me. If I could just get it on paper, I could crumple it up, burn it, throw it away, and get rid of it.

So I enrolled in a personal essay class at the New School. I'd never taken a writing class before because I'd always believed reading was what taught one how to write—but that's not why I was there. The teacher I chose was Lucy Grealy, who had just written an acclaimed memoir, *Autobiography of a Face*. A poet and essayist, Grealy had had cancer of the jaw as a child, and a torturous course of surgeries had dramatically reshaped her lovely born appearance. Until you got used to her, you could feel the residual pain, but over time she became beautiful. She had earned that face. And she ultimately helped me out of my myopic despair. She was one of the least sappy or sentimental people I'd ever met, and I was in awe of her.

Grealy's physical condition could have provided a ready excuse for any difficulty. "This singularity of meaning—I *was* my face, I *was* ugliness—though sometimes unbearable, also offered a possible point of escape," she wrote in her memoir. "It became the launching pad from which to lift off, the one immediately recognizable place to point to when asked what was wrong with my life. Everything led to it, everything receded from it—my face as personal vanishing point."

Like Grealy, I felt as if my "ugliness"—my divorce—was forcibly made visible to the rest of the world, like a scarlet D tattooed on my forehead, an affront. It felt unseemly to wear my brokenheartedness like a rebuke to other people's joy. Yet Grealy had found a way to transform her vulnerability into a source of power, turning her "ugliness" into a deeply felt work of art. I wasn't aiming anywhere that high. I just wanted the sense of exposure to disappear, to not feel like I was displaying my hurt all the time, to not allow it to define me.

The anonymity of Grealy's class was like a blanket. None of the students were professional writers. I introduced myself as a media executive at Turner Broadcasting, which, alas, I was, still finding it hard to move from marketing into pure editorial work, even as I continued to write for the *Economist* at night. A number of the students were retirees who wanted to unload what they'd learned or waited a lifetime to say, and they had little to lose. Nor did I. I didn't need to worry about what any of them thought of me or my writing. I didn't even bother to try to write well; I certainly didn't intend to publish what I wrote there, which was a torrent of raw anger and regret and sorrow—everything that had been left unsaid. I wasn't looking for readers and I absolutely did not want exposure. This was about release.

But shortly after taking the class, I decided to write about divorce again—in a very different way, and this time with a definite eye to readers. I'd recently met another woman my age who was divorced, and our bond was immediate. Listening to this new friend describe her experience, I no longer felt so alone. Soon, other divorced people in their twenties materialized where I hadn't noticed them before, and I began to seek them out. What did they know that I didn't know? What had they learned? If I could make sense of what happened to them, perhaps my own story would begin to make sense. And by writing about divorce from this broader perspective, telling other people's divorce stories, I could reach those going through the same dreadful experience. Maybe I could be their self-help. In the process, I became my own.

I began researching a book about young divorce, interviewing dozens of other divorcées for what would turn into my first book, *The Starter Marriage and the Future of Matrimony.* The people I interviewed were a good deal further along than I was; many were remarried, most at least partially healed. I lapped up their words, taking in their lessons. If they were now okay, then maybe one day I would be, too.

Right after handing in my manuscript at the end of the year 2000, I hopped on a plane to Sicily, where I cycled around the island on a group tour that consisted of four happily vacationing couples and me. On the last day of our bike trip, after three weeks of avoiding all contact with the outside world, I checked e-mail at an Internet café in Taormina. A lawyerly missive informed me that the divorce had finally gone through. It was official.

My life and Bob had been torn apart at the seams. I had swiftly fallen from the Austenian security of destined couple to the Whartonian disgrace of divorcée. But my Book of Books was still potent and full of promise, with only twenty-five of its hundred pages filled in. The binding held fast, despite the visible tears in the back. The pages I had written in before my marriage were unerasable, and the ones written in since were still part of my story. I had lots of blank pages left to go, and they were mine.

CHAPTER 16

Flashman

I Do Not Like Your Books

It's no secret that we judge other people by their books. This isn't a matter of snobbery—at least not always—but of taste and affinity and sensibility. Frankly, someone who reads only Middle English poetry and literature in translation would probably put me off as much as someone whose tastes run exclusively to westerns or historical romance. What someone reads gives you a sense of who they are. If you really don't like someone's books, chances are you probably won't like them either.

Here's my personal test case: *The Fountainhead*. I have a hard time liking someone who loves it. *Maybe* if you admire Ayn Rand's philosophy and her politics but admit the book is terribly written. Or if you hate Ayn Rand's politics but helplessly fell for the story, or it piqued your interest in architecture at an impressionable moment. But if *The Fountainhead* is one of your top five books ever, if you think it a magnificent opus of our times, a book every president—every citizen, at least those who matter!—should read, then you will probably not be my best friend.

And people judge me by my own books, for better and for worse. I once had to grit my teeth at a dinner as one person remarked, "You can always tell conservatives by the Paul Johnson on their shelves," because really, what else could those Paul Johnsons tell you? That you bought one by accident? That you'd read it out of curiosity? That it wasn't yours but was your husband's and now was your ex-husband's and somehow got left behind? That you might not always agree with everything you read, and isn't that part of the point of reading, anyway? We can misjudge each other by our book titles, too.

I certainly wouldn't want to be judged by *The Fountainhead*, which shows up in Bob, but which I read in a state of complete ignorance as bonus material for a class on twentieth-century architecture; I knew nothing of Rand or of objectivism. I even unwittingly showed it off to my French father, Bertrand, an architect but also a socialist, thinking he'd be impressed when I brought it to France to read over vacation.

"How could you bring that piece of shit into our house?" he asked in disgust.

"But it's about architecture," I replied weakly. Or was it? Within pages, I was suffering at the hands of its tyrannical main character, Howard Roark, forever plunging a fist into soil and holding forth. The lead female character, Dominique, a woman who naturally took second place to the godlike Roark, kept striding across rooms in long, columnlike gowns. Who knew why this nonsense had even been mentioned in a class about architecture, never mind how it could have sold millions of copies. I trodded on.

A hundred pages later, I was completely with Bertrand, finishing the damned thing only out of spite. I hate-read every last horrible page of *The Fountainhead* alternating between fury and despair. When it was finally over, I willfully erased it from memory, only the vague echo of Dominique, stomping around in her evening gowns, stubbornly remaining. The book went directly into the trash, where it would never hurt anyone again. Some books are just not good.

Flashman is one of those books, and had I known that, I could have saved myself a lot of time and romantic trouble. If only it had carried a warning sign: anyone who really likes this book isn't the guy for you. As soon as I read my new boyfriend Abe's copy, early in our relationship, I should have realized we were doomed. But I was in denial. After a period of gloomy postdivorce abstinence, I'd begun dating again, sorrowfully at first, and then, a few briskly aborted relationships later, with gusto. Having already met and parted ways with the One, I was eager to meet the Next One.

Abe could be it. He was ridiculously handsome and well educated and appealing. Mostly he was handsome, and I was attracted to him in a way that felt slightly unwholesome from the moment I stole him from one of my friends. To be fair, she was more a colleague than a friend (or does that make it less fair?). To be fairer, they had broken up months earlier, and she said she was "totally over it." She even had a new boyfriend. (She never spoke to me again.)

I already felt guilty because my interest in Abe dated to the

time when the two of them were still going strong. Whenever I'd
been their third wheel, I would eye him covetously, persuaded that
he was surreptitiously eyeing me, too. Generally, when I have this
kind of fantasy, it's precisely that—a fantasy. I'll think someone is
looking at me with flirtatious intent and meanwhile he's thinking something like *You look like my aunt Sylvie* or *Do you always
play with your hair?* But for once, with Abe, the wishful thinking
was real. Several months after he and my friend/colleague broke
up, he called. "I've wanted to do this for a long time," he said.

With a PhD and a law degree and I'm pretty sure one other
random master's, he was about six times better educated than I
was. He basically had a graduate degree for every time I had even
momentarily pondered and rejected the idea of going to grad
school. Surely he knew good things to read, I thought. In retro-
spect, those multiple academic credentials should have caused some
alarm.

Abe had lots of books about philosophy and law and taxes and
scuba diving and outdoor camping cookery. For fiction, he liked
the kind of masculine books I think of as naughty-upper-class-
Brit lit, the type of novels typically described as "ribald" and
"infamous" and "jolly good fun." George MacDonald Fraser's
Flashman Papers series is also, let it be noted, a favorite of British
bad boys Boris Johnson and Jeffrey Archer.

But I picked up his copy of the first *Flashman* in good spirit,
wanting to like what my new boyfriend liked. I had already read
one book by Fraser (not part of the cultish Flashman Papers), a
yellowed paperback languishing in a guesthouse in western
China. For several days it had been my sole reading companion,
and this had robbed me of any desire to pick up another Fraser
until I met Abe. Still, I needed to believe in second chances.

Flashman came with us to Belize, where Abe was initiating me into another of his preferred leisure activities, deep-sea diving. Given my troubled relationship with sports (my college application essay had been about my struggle with gym), this did not bode well. But I had fallen into that deceptive *If you love this then I must love this because I might love you* thinking. I would like Abe's books and his sports, because that's the kind of game, good sport gal I was. I had never even thought about scuba diving before, so at least I wasn't bad at it.

But scuba diving, I soon learned, is dangerous—as in, life threatening. Typically, the sharks and the boats and the storms and the poisonous eels aren't what kill you. It's your own body that does you in. The premise of scuba-diving education is that the more you read about it, the more you understand what can go wrong, the more likely you are to avoid making fatal errors underwater.

This was not my process. The more I read about scuba diving, the more frightened I got. According to the manual, you could dive too deep and too long, accumulate too much nitrogen in your body and come down with a case of nitrogen narcosis, like inhaling a megadose of laughing gas at the dentist, but not funny. You could lose your capacity for judgment and swim off oblivious into the deep sea forever. Then there was oxygen toxicity, "the bends"— just about the worst name ever given to a sports affliction with the possible exception of cauliflower ear. You could vomit underwater and you could vomit above water. You could vomit into your regulator (the device you breathe through) or your regulator could break altogether. You could bid farewell to your middle ear.

Other things could go wrong, and I contemplated all of them. If something terrible happens undersea and you panic like a normal person, you can't flee like a normal person. Instead, you have to rise methodically through the water at regular intervals (requiring math) to prevent nitrogen from proliferating in your bloodstream. Worst outcome? Death.

I tried to focus on wowing Abe with my athletic derring-do and how much I was going to love scuba diving if I didn't die. When I suppressed all of my natural anxieties and fine-tuned fears, I did end up loving it. At forty feet below, you can viscerally appreciate that the earth's topography doesn't stop at the water's edge, but continues and even amplifies below the surface. Mountains, canyons, grooved crevasses, and tunnels open before you. Schools of fish envelop you in their shimmery cumulative mass. Moray eels bray silently from within their coral cocoons, their massive jaws forming silent O's. Here is your access to a private H. G. Wellsian fantasia of half-impossible creatures.

I was fine! I didn't vomit. I didn't even feel like vomiting. It was hard to understand why anyone *would* vomit until about four days into our vacation, when someone else on our boat felt like vomiting and proceeded to do so violently and determinedly all over the boat floor and into the surrounding ocean as we hurtled toward that morning's destination. Nausea, of course, has a social element, which is one of many reasons no one likes to watch someone else throw up. You sympathize and then you empathize and then you join in.

This is nauseating? I remember thinking for a split second, watching the hapless passenger spew at my feet. My next thought was, *This is nauseating.* When we arrived at our diving destination, it felt insane to sink five feet below the surface to wait things out as you're supposed to (bobbing on the wavy surface, being, of course, nauseating). Everything in my consciousness fought against it. This is unnatural! And that was the end of my scuba-diving career. Spooked, I didn't want to dive anymore, and Abe couldn't understand why not. He had zero empathy.

So he kept diving, and I took up the lesser "sport" of snorkeling. When I retired my regulator, I could feel Abe's disappointment, his realization that I wasn't that sporty girl after all but was instead the flimsy, hypochondriacal kind of girl, one who'd imagined herself getting dengue fever on at least two previous occasions and had a persistent and abiding terror of falling down the stairs.

Abe couldn't assuage my fear because he couldn't understand it, and he most certainly couldn't empathize. In his mind, having weighed the risks and undertaken the precautions, scuba diving was an irrefutably safe endeavor. Those were the facts, and my irrational emotions flew in the face of them, disrupting his order. None of the other women he had dated had been afraid. Diving was meant to be a mutual pleasure, and I wasn't living up to expectations. He judged me, and he found me wanting.

I, in return, could say that I did not like pursuits of the person I was on vacation with. Because in addition to scuba diving, there was *Flashman*.

Yes, it's true. If we all liked the same books, we'd all boringly be the same people. That said, certain books can rightfully be considered deal breakers. In an essay in the *New York Times Book Review*, Rachel Donadio called this the Pushkin problem: "When a missed—or misguided—literary reference makes it chillingly clear that a romance is going nowhere fast." Not everyone can fall for a die-hard fan of Nicholas Sparks or a James Joyce completist.

Flashman is decidedly a cult novel, which didn't bode well. For whatever reason, when it comes to cult fiction, I'm never part of the cult. Beloved in the same way clubby Wodehouse is beloved but by fewer people, *Flashman*, published in 1969, is the first in a series whose subsequent titles each felt like a slap in the face (e.g., *Flashman and the Redskins*, *Flashman's Lady*). The cover of *Flashman* Volume I featured a swaggering bloke in uniform with a bare-breasted maiden of "exotic" background, in, of course, the background. Sometimes you *can* tell a book by its cover.

Here's what Abe loved so much: the title character, Harry Paget Flashman, a faux historical Zelig-like figure, romps across the British Empire, landing variously in Scotland, India, and Afghanistan. Sprinkled throughout are minor figures from British history—Lord Auckland, governor-general of India for a spell; Paolo di Avitabile, a governor of Peshawar province; Thomas Arnold, headmaster at the Rugby School; and the like. But the main draw is its rogue protagonist, a light dragoon and a womanizing drunkard who skips from duel to romp to "forceful seduction." Most of the time, he frequents prostitutes, but he also enjoys raping an Afghan dancing girl. I have nothing against a good antihero, but I didn't even enjoy hating this guy. I just wanted to get away from him.

There can certainly be pleasure in hate reading. As with *The Fountainhead*, I have hated my way through several books to the last page, not always out of generosity to the writer. It's a force of will. You will be read no matter how hard you make it. Some say reading hateful books feels like time wasted—and with so little time, so many books, why bother with the bad? But there's something bracing about reading a book you despise, because loathing is usually mixed with other emotions—fear, perverse attraction, even occasional, complicated strains of sympathy. It's one of many reasons I believe in negative reviews. It can be interesting when a book provokes animosity. But hate in and of itself is not a very interesting response to a book, and, oh, how I hated *Flashman*.

My distaste didn't ruffle Abe in the least. Sure, it was a failing on my part, but for the most part he didn't care. This sanguinity in the face of my displeasure seemed to imply a kind of passivity or, more distressingly, an absence of passion. In the course of our relationship, I discovered William Dean Howells and read him voraciously; Abe had no interest. I read George Eliot's *Adam Bede* (no interest) and Cathi Hanauer's anthology *The Bitch in the House* (need I even say).

The absence of mutual engagement felt like a loss. Reading together is a way to bond. It's nice when people like the books you like. There's even a joy in finding someone else who hates the same book as much as you do. There were books I longed to discuss and dissect and even debate, books I would have argued about with my ex-husband in a pattern I found reassuring and rewarding. But Abe had no truck with me on any of them. When I thought about it, he didn't really engage with me as a person at all; I was merely a foil. We were not on the same page.

And so I broke up with him. I decided to mark the rupture with a long solo road trip from the Grand Canyon, through the national parks of Utah, over to Las Vegas, where I'd never been, and then to California, where I'd follow the Pacific Coast Highway from Los Angeles to my brother Roger's apartment in San Francisco. I would clear my head and get back to what *I* wanted to do. I would read whatever I wanted at night and listen in the car to whatever books I wanted by day, and make up my own company without someone else's indifference simmering in the background. I may have had no one to talk to about any of it, but at least I had no one to make me feel bad about having no one to talk to. Four years after my divorce, I was okay with that.

Yet the breakup seemed to arouse an unfamiliar passion in Abe, who protested the entire plan. "The trip will be much better if I come along," he insisted. He'd been to the Grand Canyon and knew how to see it. He knew the national parks. He'd bring his lightweight camping equipment and would cook gourmet meals over a Bunsen burner. He got very excited about how lightly you could camp and how well you could eat while doing so. This was another of his favorite things, and another of his favorite things that left me cold. But Abe was adamant. We should get back together and this trip would show why.

So Abe came. I regretted caving almost immediately; his lack of interest in everything from the audiobooks to the scenery to me sapped energy out of the entire endeavor. He sighed lightly as I popped in an audiobook of Edmund Morris's controversial biography of Ronald Reagan, *Dutch*, wanting to hear firsthand Morris's lightly fictionalized account, in which he, the biographer, created a stand-in character to represent himself. Had it really been a terrible decision? Discuss.

Abe had no opinion. He didn't want to talk about the book or about Morris or about the biographer's responsibility or the opaqueness of Ronald Reagan. Nor did Abe talk about the cacti, the Painted Desert, the monumental stone edifices of Zion National Park. Everything got swallowed up in his apathy. By the time we got to California, I was doubly sure we were over.

In San Francisco, I saw my closest friend from college, Victoria. Vic was my most sensible friend—down-to-earth, loyal, zero tolerance for pretension or condescension. She'd been one of the few people I'd known in college who wasn't afraid to call out other people on their bullshit. That night, I pulled her aside to ask her a burning question. Vic had been on the swim team in college; she was not afraid of the water.

"Have you ever gone scuba diving?" I asked.

"Are you fucking kidding me?" she said. "I would *never*. It's extremely dangerous for one thing and, besides that, it's terrifying." Sure, go and swim across a pool or a lake, lovely; but swimming while under thousands of tons of water was nuts. If I had only known of Vic's claustrophobic aversion, I wouldn't have felt like such an outlier in Belize, such a terrible disappointment. Here was a college swim team champion, and she wanted nothing to do with scuba diving either, dammit.

But it was too late now, and oddly irrelevant. There was no longer any issue between Abe and me, not about scuba diving, not about *Flashman*, not about lightweight camping, not about us. There was no parting of the minds because there had never been a meeting of the minds, nor of the heart. Like a reader and character completely out of sync, we had zero empathy for each other. When we went our separate ways, both my heart and my Book of Books remained blessedly intact.

CHAPTER 17

The Master and Margarita

Recommendations

"You should read this book" almost never simply means you should read this book. It is usually far more fraught. Telling someone what to read, even asking politely, can feel more like an entreaty or an implied judgment or a there's-something-you-should-know than a straightforward proposal. If you read this book, then you love me. If you read this book, then you respect my opinions. If you read this book, you will understand what it is I need you to understand and can't explain to you myself.

What might be about shared enthusiasm and appreciation can even weirdly become a kind of threat. If you read this book, then you'd know better. If you're smart, you'll read this. Or you have to be smart to read this, and you're a fool if you don't. Everyone else is reading this. Everyone else already has.

There's good reason to take book recommendations person-ally, even when they have more to do with the person doing the recommending than with the person on the receiving end of the suggestion. With my brother Roger, for example, book recom-mendations were imperatives that one needed to heed, and I wasn't sure I'd be his sister anymore if I didn't listen.

Roger had trained me to follow his lead early on. When we were little, he lorded over our younger brother Brian and me, and whenever we violated one of his codes, his right index finger would shoot high into the air in a brutal display of power.

"Suspennnnsion!" he'd announce, drawing out the second syllable as if to savor our anguish.

"What's the suspension? What's the suspension?" Brian and I would babble, frantic.

"One week, no Atari," Roger would say with cool matter-of-factness, as if he'd just consulted the rule book. "One week, no *Monster Manual.*" "No comic books." And later, O bitterness: "No Apple II Plus." Whatever we had done wrong, we had to be punished. Taking out the garbage for a few days might get us out of it, but that was scary—it was dark, and there were raccoons.

As he got older, Roger's laws transitioned from not letting me touch any of his books to foisting his books upon me. If I didn't follow his bidding, there would be trouble. One weekend, we had to go to a bar mitzvah in Colorado. "Read this now," he said when we got there, handing me a copy of John Kennedy Toole's *A Confederacy of Dunces.* "I don't want to speak to you until you're done."

I read it. There was no need to threaten; I trusted him. When Roger read *The Red and the Black* his freshman year at Bard, I read *The Red and the Black* my sophomore year in high school, ever desperate to follow his lead and to please him. The effort would invariably be rewarded. Roger knew a good book, which I knew because I'd been secretly swiping his books for a long time. I read his junior novelization of *Jaws* when I wasn't allowed to see the movie. I extracted *Go Ask Alice* from under his bed when he wasn't home. Though I was only supposed to touch the *Monster Manual* and *Deities & Demigods*, which had already been sullied by overuse, I would read the forbidden *Dungeon Master's Guide* as well and then replace it in precisely the place where I'd found it, as if nothing had happened.

In the year 2000, to celebrate the new millennium, I made a deal with Roger, one in which I, for once, would dictate the book. If he read *War and Peace*, I would read *War and Peace*, and, as a reward, I would fly the two of us to Russia for a vacation. There, we would discuss the Bezukhovs and the Bolkonskys, the Rostovs and the Kuragins, the Drubetskoys and Napoleon and Waterloo and whether it was better than *Anna Karenina* (which he'd told me to read years earlier) while hurtling by train from Moscow to St. Petersburg.

Roger had long been my comrade in arms when it came to Russian literature. On a trip to Portland to visit our cousin Kirsten, he shoved into my hands Mikhail Bulgakov's Soviet-era satire *The Master and Margarita*. "We'll talk when you're done," he'd said. And because I respected his taste and possibly because I still feared his suspensions, I obeyed. After reading the love story of the imprisoned author the Master and his devoted, besotted Margarita, I passed it on to Kirsten, sealing the familial bond. In Russia, I would be able to repay Roger as we walked through Patriarch Ponds and checked out the graffiti on Bulgakov House, reimagining scenes in which the devil comes to Moscow.

I was really doing Roger a favor. Everyone intends to read *War and Peace* eventually, and the Russia trip gave us an excuse. Roger would read his copy in San Francisco, and I would read mine in New York. I'd tried reading it several years earlier and given up around page one hundred, lost. This time, I bought an edition with a crucial addition: a family tree. Aided by this handy patronymic road map, I could be swept into the narrative without forgetting who everyone was.

The secret that Russian literature aficionados somehow manage to keep from the rest of the world, daunted by names like Dostoyevsky and Turgenev, is that Russian novels are essentially soap operas. Sure, there's the backdrop of the nineteenth century to contend with, but at heart Russian novels are stories of unrequited love, lusty affairs, and die-hard feuds. Even the long ones can feel too short. *War and Peace* would be no problem.

"I'm on it," Roger told me every time I called to make sure he was keeping up his end of the bargain. Deep into the novel myself, I knew Roger would also love it. We both reveled in the darkly gleeful slapstick of Russian satire. I see myself in every lowly and ill-used clerk from Kovalyov to Golyadkin, and my brother does, too. Anything he laughs at, I laugh at, and vice versa.

I tore through *War and Peace* that month, and come March we set off for the motherland. Everything was going according to plan. I couldn't wait to talk over our Tolstoy.

"I didn't read it," Roger confessed once the plane reached cruising altitude. "But I meant to."

I should have known. Except in cases of rare devotion—and even then—trying to make someone read something is like force-feeding a baby. Most people prefer reading what they want to read. This cold fact was particularly upsetting to my father, who viewed reading or watching something he recommended as a demonstration, even a proof, of love. He was obsessed with recommending, cajoling over and over until you submitted. "You have to watch *Ballad of a Soldier*, he'd insist, strong-arming you into the TV room. "Come in here," he'd say as soon as I walked into his apartment on the Upper West Side. "I just want to show you one scene from *Black Narcissus*. Just one scene! *Pammy, please!*"

These repeated requests only hardened my lack of interest. I'm not sure why, as his recommendations tended to be worthy, and the palpable joy my mutual enjoyment elicited was its own reward. But I would dig in my heels. Perhaps it was because when I was a child, reading had been my way to declare independence. Perhaps because I too wanted to read what I wanted to read. Watch what I wanted to watch. Choose my own adventures.

"You're never going to make your father happy and watch *The Red Shoes*, are you?" he'd ask miserably. "Can't you just sit through the opening sequence?" When I started dating, he took to asking my boyfriends instead, where his chances of success were greater. "Have you ever seen *Stalingrad*?" he'd ask, throwing a paternal arm over some poor guy's shoulder. "Let me show you the opening scene of *The Loneliness of the Long Distance Runner*."

With books, he was slightly less demanding. I'd see him spread out an illustrated guide to field artillery before one of my decidedly nonmilitaristic boyfriends—like he was sharing a rite of manhood—and plot a rescue operation. He didn't employ these same tactics with me. It may be he knew I wouldn't cotton to Robert Ludlum ("They're not good," he admitted) or David Baldacci ("These are really terrible, Pammy—but I enjoy them"). My father was an unself-conscious reader, in it for his own pleasure and curiosity, something I, with my studious aspirations and constant looking over my shoulder, envied. He read voraciously, plunging into a subject and dwelling there for years. From Catskills history to old graveyards to the Spanish Civil War, where he embedded himself for well over a decade, supplementing his reading material with folk music and undercover visits to meetings of veterans of the Lincoln Brigade. ("These people are crazy, Pammy! But I find them fascinating.")

My new boyfriend Michael was the same way with his books. He read high, he read low, he read in the middle. He read according to whim and mood and passing interest and passion. He read a lot of books I'd never heard of, something I always find especially alluring. And our curiosity about and interest in each other was mutual. When we met, I was reading Benjamin Franklin's autobiography; he was reading Robert K. Massie's *Dreadnought*. We looked at each other's books and thought, *We're good!*

Shortly into our courtship, I left for Germany on a three-week trip I'd been planning for months but now wished I weren't doing solo. In Frankfurt, I'd be staying with college friends who were working in finance; in Heidelberg, I'd visit my French sister, Juliette, there on a postdoctoral fellowship in biogenetics. I had a magazine story to write in Baden-Baden (hardship assignment on the city's storied baths). Everything had been carefully mapped out, but already I felt like someone was missing.

At every village with an Internet café, I stopped to check for messages from Michael. I thought about what he would think when we returned together to those very same spots one day. Would he also love the museum of advertising? Would he marvel at the wooded twists of the Alpenstrasse? The few moments not devoted to what he thought were spent thinking about what our children would think and how much they would like the cuckoo clock museum.

When I got back to New York, I had my usual Bob update to do: I entered the books I'd read on my trip, a random assortment of paperbacks given to me by a friend who worked in publishing, into my Book of Books. And then I found myself thinking about a literary present I wanted to give to Michael (I'd brought back only a small matchbox from Germany, from a *guesthaus* bearing his family name). This was a coup, but the next gift would be more meaningful. A few weeks later, sitting on a bench in Central Park one night, I presented him with a small wrapped package containing three books: *Middlemarch*, because I adored George Eliot and was making my way through her entire oeuvre (still not *Romola*, I must confess). *Buddenbrooks*, because I was determined to keep Thomas Mann as my own rather than allow him to become a relic of my ex-husband. And *The Master and Margarita*, because my brother had passed it to me and I'd passed it to Kirsten, and I felt fairly certain that Michael was soon to be part of this circle. I inscribed each of them with messages.

These three books weren't my favorites. Nor did I expect Michael to read them right away. It just seemed that if I were going to get involved with someone and he were going to get involved with me, he should get a sense of what moved me on the page. I wanted to please him and for him to be pleased by me. The prospect of finding someone who takes as much pleasure in the book as I do is often more a reward than the book itself. A little like my dad, after all.

To my astonishment, Michael began reading right away. He didn't like the books nearly as much as I did and his take-aways often differed radically from my own. But that was okay—

he wanted to know about what I read and what I thought. He later went on to buy me a replacement set of Mann's *Joseph and His Brothers* and a beautiful edition of George Eliot's letters. My books, my life of the mind and of the heart, meant something to him. And his did to me. Michael's shelves were stocked with contemporary British novelists I'd never heard of, long-forgotten fiction from the 1970s, books about computer hackers and mountain-climbing accidents, polemics about civil liberties, and outdated computer manuals.

There was nothing I would have read on my own in the past and a lot of it I had no desire to read in the future. But his books showed a very different mind at work. I didn't know what to expect from this person, and in a dating world that can feel wearyingly predictable, this was exciting.

When Michael gave a toast at our wedding, he pointed out that I'd given him "a reading list" early on in our relationship.

> Chief amongst these was George Eliot's *Middlemarch*, and as you can imagine I read the book with a particular interest in determining what characters, or episodes, or deft turns of phrase had made her so recommend this book to me . . .
> Book two on the list was Bulgakov's *The Master and Margarita*. This was more encouraging. It is the story of, among other things, a beautiful woman who falls for a guy who gets arrested and then hides himself in an insane asylum for years so as not to embarrass her . . . In the words of Bulgakov, "Love caught us suddenly, leapt at us like a murderer appearing from nowhere in an alley, and struck us both down at once.

Like lightning, like a Finnish knife! However, afterwards she insisted it was not so, that we had loved each other for a long, long time, without knowing one another, never having met..."

The toast went on—not just about the books I'd given him, but about everything I'd given him so far and everything he'd given me and what we both planned to give each other in the future. He ended with a quote from *Great Expectations*. What could I say? I was humbled and I was dazzled and I was sure. Shortly after we'd met, I introduced Michael to Bob, and he came up with his own variation, the Blob—Big List of Books—which he put on his computer. Not long after that, he entered *Buddenbrooks* into his Big List of Books. He keeps his Blob still.

CHAPTER 18

The Hunger Games

No Time to Read

I'd just given birth after a long and well-medicated labor that ended with my second son, Theodore. He was an unexpectedly immense nine-and-a-half-pound baby, fat and uncomplaining. My recovery was swift. This was my third child and the easiest of my childbirths. Most mothers would have bolted from the hospital, especially if their two other children at home were still rather young. But I chose to stay an extra day.

I wish I could say it was because I worried that the new baby's siblings, Tobias and Beatrice, two and four years old respectively, would steal attention away from him. But this would not be completely honest. In truth, I stayed in the hospital because I was in the middle of *The Hunger Games*. I'd started reading it in early labor, paused so that I could give birth, and then picked it back up to read almost immediately after Teddy was born and latched on, reading as I nursed. It was a genuine page-turner, and for once, with great pleasure, I had time to turn the pages.

Nobody could interrupt to ask for a snack. Nobody needed me to wrestle with a shoe. I didn't have to furrow my brow through background shrieks of wants and needs, or anticipate who would ask next for help tracking down a misplaced lovey. I hadn't read like this for years.

Glued to the story of teenagers murdering each other for survival, I hardly noticed whether Teddy ate or slept. When will the rebellion begin, I wanted to know. Which suitor would the killer heroine Katniss choose? It was *fine* for me to turn my attention to these matters. This was my third child and I knew what I was doing, babywise. I expertly breastfed him as I raced through the pages with one finger, each of us occupied and contented. It wasn't until halfway through the final book in the trilogy that I realized Teddy was taking an awfully long time to tank up. Turns out, he hadn't been latched on properly the entire time. And here I was reading a book called *The Hunger Games*! Once I put the book down, I returned to my resting emotional state of maternal guilt.

These lunatic years of turbo lactivism, nursing my children until they were weaned, were tainted not by formula but by the competing desire to read while they fed. Breast-feeding your children can be a beautiful, bonding experience when it does not involve undue pain or inconvenience. But let me be clear: it is *also* a perfect time for reading, the mom version of dad hanging out on the toilet with an iPad. Everything about breastfeeding lends itself to the practice. The dedicated nursing pillows prop up books as well as they do babies. The baby, staring off into the middle distance, doesn't seem bothered and may even be enjoying the story in some way. Oxytocin, the "love hormone," leaves the nursing mother unusually calm and focused. I felt the stories more.

This nurse-reading opportunity made itself known early on. A few months after my first child was born, I was working from home as a freelancer, taking a self-imposed "maternity leave" from writing books and chasing down magazine and newspaper assignments, when an editor at the *New York Times Book Review* asked me to review a book. It was supposed to be my time off, but since I was the one giving and taking that time, the rules behind this policy were distinctly loose. I read the e-mail request, then looked over at Beatrice. She was zonked out peacefully in her bassinet, a real sleeper. This was an infant who slumbered by our side even as Michael and I watched *Black Hawk Down* at full volume twelve inches away. "Sure," I e-mailed back. "Send it over."

The book arrived and it was charming, *The Lady and the Panda*, which told the story of Ruth Harkness and her efforts to bring the first panda bear from China to America, a tale distinguished by a complicated heroine, adorable baby pandas, and a tragic ending. Over this absorbing narrative, I learned how to balance my daughter on my nursing pillow, prop up my book, and blissfully engage with both. The review was glowing.

Two years later, another baby, another e-mail from the *Book Review*. "Sure," I wrote back, glancing contentedly at Tobias, only four weeks old and fast asleep.

The book arrived and Tobias woke up, as babies are wont to do after those first deceptively somnolent weeks. He promptly issued a whole set of demands. He would sleep only if tightly swaddled with arms immobilized, and at the same time and rather determinedly, he would sleep only swaddle-free, his arms swinging wildly overhead. Or, two minutes later, he would sleep only if I laid him across my lap and sat still and silent and yet somehow, at the same time, only while I held him aloft, cradling him back and forth with a knee-bending sway, cooing rhythmically. I scrambled to keep up with his shifting parameters, double guessing and waiting for maternal know-how to arrive at a definitive solution.

Meanwhile, the assigned book for review was a stew of political theory mumbo jumbo as written by a team of second-rate grad students. When Tobias wasn't wailing at me for not sleeping him right, I was scowling at the terrible book. Every moment, baby or book, was a misery. I wrote a scathing review. My editor assured me I'd done readers a service. People have limited time for books, and the job of reviewers is to help them make choices.

Most people in the throes of parenting have little time to read. Instead, time is spent strategizing how to meet the barest requirements of adulthood, with reading a vice snuck on the sly like an afternoon cocktail. My lifelong requirement to read before bed, no matter how late the hour and preceded by a vastly underestimating "I just need to read one page," now actually often ends at exactly that: one page. So much energy is expended dashing frantically from task to task that the sporadic slap to the forehead, "I forgot about Bob!" has escalated in frequency. By the time I remember to note a book in his pages, I sometimes have to struggle to remember the title. Twenty minutes more sleep at night would surely enhance that ability. But who has time for that?

There's nothing unusual about the no-time-for-books complaint, but it feels like a fireable offense when reading is your job. Publishers, editors, authors, fellow readers know you can't read everything, but expect it anyway. I kind of expect it, too. If I tell someone I'm going to read a book, I do. It's that hard-to-shake feeling that someone will ferret out the lapse if you don't. "You there," I half expect someone to corner me and say. "What did you make of chapter seven?" Half my book-related conversations seem to begin with someone asking, "Have you read X or Y book?" followed by a doleful, "No, have you?"

Also, I read worse. Some studies allege that child rearing makes people smarter, that we learn to anticipate dangers that operate at the .001 percent level of likelihood, to perform Olympic feats of multitasking, to jump in with adrenaline surges of mastery when necessary. I'm not so sure. Each additional child has only weakened my base multitasking skills and frayed my attention span. I have less time and energy to devote to abstract thought. Sleeplessness seems to have worn the bearings of an already faulty memory, child after child after child chipping away at what once was known. There's a too-true Roz Chast cartoon about the aging brain's incapacities: whenever new information goes in (tabloid gossip), something must go out (algebra). The accumulating necessities of small children—the checkups, orthodontic visits, outgrown shoes, broken bones, surgeries, convalescences—take a brutal toll, withering my mental capacity in sad counterpoint to my children's elastic and expanding minds.

At least kids force you to prioritize. You learn to let go of the bad books more easily and savor the good. Each moment becomes a calculation, and there is always an opportunity cost. Rather than spend this time reading dreck, what could you be doing instead?

When Beatrice was four months old, I went on tour for my second book, and she came along. I'd pass her to my mother as I stood swaying from lack of sleep in front of bookstore audiences, unable to find my place in my own book or to recognize the text within as something I'd been remotely involved in. Next, Beatrice accompanied me to Washington. My husband and I had driven down so I could testify before Congress about my research on the very child-unfriendly subject of pornography. By then Beatrice was a fairly reasonable six-month-old. But so preoccupied was I with the pumping of milk and the timing of the nap and the questionable opacity of the window shades in the hotel room that it wasn't until my husband deposited me in front of the Capitol that I realized I'd neglected to prepare my testimony.

Here I was, about to talk about hard-core pornography in the halls of Congress. Senator Sam Brownback was sponsoring me, and Senator Orrin Hatch, forever imprinted in my mind holding a copy of *The Exorcist* during the Anita Hill–Clarence Thomas hearings, was there, too. It felt like some kind of diabolical dream sequence, but it was real and it was up to me to wing it. Months later, after the fog of early motherhood lifted, I picked up a photograph taken that day of me, surrounded by senators. I was wearing a miniskirt, which basically isn't allowed in Washington, and an inappropriately enormous smile, eyes dazed. I vaguely recall having a deeply personal conversation with Sam Brownback about his men's group.

Now that I had three small children, the number of books I pick up has dropped precipitously, and, with it, the number of books I put down completed. My Book of Books is a rather unkind reminder of this. Though I didn't think to enumerate my entries in Bob until the list was well into the three hundreds, once I did, the enterprise was unavoidably tarnished. How can you not feel smug about the growing tally? How can you not be eager to add yet another number to the list?

But therein lies danger. The numbers do not, alas, tick upward at a steady rate, and you can easily gauge just how much you've "fallen behind." Have you read as many books this March as you did last? What's your yearly average? What of the long books that slow you down: *Vanity Fair, Hamilton, The Pickwick Papers*? Could they not somehow count doubly?

Graphic novels, illustrated works, Dover thrift editions, Penguin 60s, reread books: all of this can feel like cheating. (Even I draw the line at picture books, which do not make it into Bob, much as it would favor the average.) It would be dishonest to deny that part of me sometimes wants to just finish a book already, especially a bad one, so I can move up another digit on my way to the next even hundred.

These ambitions aside, Bob reflects an inexorable decline, its rate dropping in response to accumulated responsibilities, children birthed and tended, piled-up magazines, the dumb side of the Internet. Now, when I should be reading, I find myself instead gazing at baby pictures on my phone or scrolling through Twitter bytes instead. In the year after college graduation, when I was living in Thailand, I read seventy-six books, including whoppers like *Moby-Dick*, aided considerably by a sporadic level of employment. The following year, in New York and fully employed, the number slipped to thirty-four. Early on, a boyfriend had criticized me for tallying my books and I had balked. Bob and I had nothing to prove! But the truth was, it did matter. My private reading life, as many aspects of private life after parenthood, can easily slip away.

With reading time curtailed, page-turners become a form of punishment. What was once a delicious abandonment to plot, a desperation to finish yet at the same time a rationing to prolong the ecstasy, to please not let it end quite yet, has become something else entirely: a nightmare. A masochistic thrumming of simultaneous desire and deprivation involving late nights and little sleep, ignored and resentful children, furtive retreats into the bathroom to secretly flip the pages. Like cheating.

That was *The Hunger Games*, a joy and pain. And the way of all top-tier genre—quasi-vampires and spy novels and plot-twisty, mind-sucking domestic thrillers that have to be finished right now without interruption—even when your entire life is interruption. Trilogies or series of any kind, life destroying. Reading is transformed from life's central act to a secret second (or even third) life that your *real* life isn't allowed to know about. Books become compartmentalized rather than integral.

These days I fit reading in on a catch-as-catch-can basis, even as I've exorcised most other distractions from my cultural diet. I read about TV more than I watch it. My movie viewing is nearly all animated. Books gnaw at me from around the edges of my life, demanding more time and attention. I am always left hungry.

CHAPTER 19

A Wrinkle in Time

Reading with Children

Certain periods of your life become inextricably linked with certain books. For me, even as I continued to read books for myself, the early child-rearing years were about children's books, both my kids' and my own. This was a time of revisiting and rereading and reliving the stories that had remained with me, if in the back of my brain, since my first days as a reader. Those simple yet oddly indelible story lines and the intense emotions they elicit: Leo Lionni's *Little Blue and Little Yellow*, which makes you realize even as a child that a relationship can compromise your identity, even make you unrecognizable. Or Maurice Sendak's *Where the Wild Things Are*, which alerts you to the power of your own anger, capable of sending you reeling into another world, one from which you'd have to find your way back.

To witness feelings you've only experienced within reflected in the pages of a book is a revelation. The sense memory of those initial reading experiences resurge in a visceral way and, for an odd time-suspended moment, you can actually see what the pages looked like through your six-year-old eyes, a feeling Spalding Gray called "a complicated present"—one in which you are both in the present and in the past at the same time.

Those early books become imprinted on us like a cherished stuffed animal or maternal embrace. They become part of us, belong to us in a way they don't belong to anyone else. "Even now, simply thinking about Long John Silver or the waves on Crusoe's island stirs me far more than reading the original text," J. G. Ballard once said. "I suspect that these childhood tales have long since left their pages and taken on a second life inside my head."

That is the awesome power of children's literature, and children are in power here. Teachers may be able to tell you what to do in school and parents can control what you do at home, whether you get to watch TV and whether you can play at Jenny's house two days in a row. You may not be allowed to see a PG movie or use the phone after ten o'clock at night. But books are different. From a very young age, most children get to select the books they read or acquiesce to listening to while read by another. Even before you fully learn to read on your own, you are the one who decides which stories to let in.

Most kids weigh this decision by parsing the freighted cues of cover, illustration, title, and endorsements. It's what makes book jackets so essential during childhood, when in choosing a book outside the purview of the parent or the teacher or the librarian, the prospective reader has little else to go on. Go on the Internet and search for the covers of your childhood favorites; you'll recognize "your" covers immediately, each one like a personalized invitation. Is it intimidating or inviting? Are the characters aspirational or relatable? Are you going to entrust this book, this author, with your time? When you pick up a book, Doris Lessing once said, "you are about to enter the mind of someone who thinks differently from yourself." That requires consideration.

It is no small decision. You, young reader, determine location. You pick your company. You elect which world you enter and what knowledge you procure there. While subject to the author's whims should you continue reading, you can also reject them and put the book down.

In my Book of Books, I can see the way these choices line up and read the signs along the way that reveal those decisions. Here, a novel selected with deliberation; the next, a matter of circumstance. This one was assigned, but that one a book I was dying to read. My mother-in-law gave me that book. This other one was found in the common room of a New England bed-and-breakfast. All of those choices.

Choosing a book is so gratifying, it's worth dragging out the process, starting even before finishing the current one. As the final chapters approach, you can pile up the possibilities like a stack of travel brochures. You can lay out three books and let them linger overnight before making a final decision in the morning. You can Google the reviews; ask other people if they've read it, collect information. The choice may ultimately depend on the mood and the moment. "You have to read a book at the right time for you," Lessing also said, "and I am sure this cannot be insisted on too often, for it is the key to the enjoyment of literature."

And so, the eager new parent thinks, we can pass on that enjoyment to our children. Every night, read-aloud time becomes an extension of the reader's power. We not only get to pick our own books, we get to pick our children's books as well. We point them to the good ones. We instruct them in how to read clues on the jacket. We show them how it's done. They will be good readers, lucky them and lucky us: the culture now values children who read.

I spent a lifetime planning for this. I even had a head start, having begun collecting books for my kids before they were born. I started by stashing away a few key titles while working at Scholastic when I was 100 percent single. My children would never want for books. I'd pass by a bookstore and pick up a few Dr. Seusses on sale figuring, *One day, I'm going to need these.* I'd find a copy of a beloved childhood favorite in a used bookstore, *Miss Suzy* or *The Story of Ferdinand* or *Richard Scarry's Busy Town*, and purchase it for my nonexistent children.

Once those children actually existed, they made it quite clear that this planning was for naught. I didn't have that bonus you-will-read-this power, it turned out—at least not for long. Given the choice (and they were given the choice), they wanted to decide on the books themselves, as I should have well known. They wanted to hear godawful Biscuit books instead of *Make Way for Ducklings.* They thought *Alice's Adventures in Wonderland* was boring. They didn't like homey animal stories or books about trees. They weren't as beguiled as I was by the prospect of unlimited black-and-white blueberries.

The ability to choose one's own books becomes slightly less satisfying when you realize your own children have that power, too, and they insist on reading about rainbow fairies or killer cats. You can momishly lead a child in certain directions—point him to particular shelves at the library, refuse to buy certain books, discuss treasured authors in favorable terms and hope he doesn't hear about the others. But those techniques take you only so far. I was shocked when, after handing my ten-year-old daughter a fiftieth-anniversary boxed set of Madeleine L'Engle's *A Wrinkle in Time* quintet (still but a wee trilogy in my youth), she stopped after the first book. "Don't you want to continue to *A Wind in the Door*?" I asked, scandalized.

For girls who came of age anytime during the past half century, reading L'Engle's Newbery Medal–winning classic was pivotal. The main character, Meg Murry, offered a real departure from the typical "girls' book" protagonist—as wonderful as many of those varied characters are. Here was an awkward child whose flyaway hair, braces, and glasses existed alongside a fierce intelligence and determination, which she uses to save her father, and ultimately the universe. She reaches girls just as they are actively seeking to define themselves, their own ambitions, and their place in the world, and shows them a way that has nothing to do with looks or popularity or submission.

I had bestowed upon my daughter a sacred nugget of maternal wisdom, and she had cast it aside.

In 1962, when *A Wrinkle in Time* was acquired by the publisher Farrar, Straus & Giroux after it had been rejected twenty-six times, science fiction aimed at girls was a rarity. The stuff of pulp and comics for errant schoolboys, sci-fi was not considered up to the standards of children's literature. Even today, girls and grown women are not often fans. Half of eighteen- to twenty-four-year-old men say science fiction is their favorite kind of book, compared with only a fourth of young women. And while a sizable portion of young men continue to read science fiction into later adulthood, women generally don't.

A Wrinkle in Time defied the norm by inviting girls in and valuing them. The story follows three children as they cross the barriers of time and space through something called a tesseract. On a "dark and stormy night," Mrs Whatsit (whose honorific appeared mysteriously without periods), a celestial being disguised as an old woman, visits Meg; her mother, a microbiologist who later wins the Nobel Prize; and her younger brother, Charles Wallace. Soon Meg and Charles Wallace, a prodigy of sorts— today he might be considered on the spectrum—and Calvin O'Keefe, a high school boy, are tesseracting across the universe in search of Meg's father.

Meg can perform square-root functions in her head, a mark not of wallflower status but of moral distinction. Still, she harbors doubts about her intellectual abilities, and her exacting expectations rub off on the reader. Yet it's Meg, a girl who combines both the ordinary and the extraordinary, who overcomes the book's villain—an evil disembodied brain called IT—with the power of a simple human emotion. At its core, *A Wrinkle in Time* is about love, a girl's love for her parents, and her ability to marshal her strengths to rescue and honor them. I desperately wanted Beatrice to see herself in that book and to love it.

She did not. If part of the inevitable maturation of the parent is to realize how different one's children are from oneself, a corollary is realizing one's children may not appreciate the same books either. As my kids got older, the evening's read-aloud time shifted to parallel reading. They read their books, and I read mine. I laugh now that I could have ever imagined otherwise.

Like Beatrice, I've always jealously guarded my freedom to

choose my own books; I've never wanted to *have* to read a book, whether for work or for play. This is why, throughout my twenties and well into my thirties, I resisted joining a book club, despite longing for a community of readers. What if they chose the wrong book or stole me away from mine?

Then I discovered Kidlit, a children's book club, or, more precisely, a book club for adults exclusively devoted to children's literature. The books were easy to read, and they were short. They were also, during this period, central to my life, given my three young children. The members of Kidlit, not all of whom even had children, firmly believed children's books should be central throughout your life. Now *this* might work.

I got involved in Kidlit through my friend Gretchen, whom I met in that layered almost conspiratorial way that often happens in New York, via several channels simultaneously. First, I spotted her at an evening salon for women, in which prominent writers were invited to speak to a small group every month or so. Gretchen seemed to know everyone there. Later, I realized she was a fellow mother at Beatrice's summer camp. There, too, she knew everyone. Finally, we were introduced at a party, and the various intersections coalesced into friendship.

It turned out Gretchen also knew everyone who loved Kidlit. She and her friend Jen, a literary agent, had started the book club when they realized that as adults they both needed to talk about Harry Potter. Not only did they like reading Potter, they liked reading all children's books, whether written for starry-eyed eight-year-olds or sullen eighteen-year-olds. And they weren't alone. By the time I joined the group, the group had over a dozen members and had spawned an offshoot. (There are now three branches.) Every six weeks, we would gather over dinner to discuss a children's book, rotating among classic (*Little House on the Prairie*), modern (*Island of the Blue Dolphins*), and contemporary (*The Fault in Our Stars*) literature.

Kidlit offered something I'd never had before outside of Paris—a place to get together regularly with fellow readers (most of them far better read than I) to discuss books I cared passionately about, without call for embarrassment or excuse. Even when the books were intended for children. Here were my people! Nobody judged anyone else, even as our opinions on particular titles wildly diverged. We argued over whether Katniss was a tool of the state, and whether *The Hunger Games* was a conventional romance or a subversion of the genre.

All of us took children's literature seriously. And we had fun. Unlike a lot of grown-up novels, children's books never lose sight of the primacy of storytelling. Children like to be swept up right away in plot, and frankly, most adults appreciate this too; it's why so many readers gravitate toward spy novels and science fiction and thrillers, books in which things happen and people get caught up in those events. It is, after all, children's books that turn us into readers in the first place.

But the best children's books also encourage young people to ask big questions about who they are and what their place is in the world. When you read children's literature as an adult, you get to revisit the same sense of newness and discovery that you did as a child. You can delve into big emotions, without cynicism or jadedness. You let all that go. In my Book of Books, the entries for children's literature don't stop after adolescence; they continue throughout, whether read for myself or with my children.

Bonding over children's books feels like an especially emotional experience; it's one of the many things that makes parent-child

reading so delicious. Nothing really compares with mutual appreciation with a child who is just embarking on a lifetime of reading. Happily, despite differences in opinion, Beatrice and I share
certain literary tastes. Beatrice is also drawn to dark tales—the
grimmer the Grimms, the better. She and I read endless incarna-
tions of fairy tales, taking apart the different renditions—was the
witch banished or did she meet a gruesome end?—and mulling
the implications together.

Beatrice and I also like stories with morals. We don't look
much alike physically, but seeing that same yearning for dark reading while wanting clear rules was like finding myself reflected
back in the glint of my daughter's eyes. She and I share a nostalgic streak, something I, too, had from a young age when I yearned
for the days of Abigail Adams. Laura Ingalls Wilder's Little House
books, which I read to Beatrice when she was in third grade (after
tours through Narnia and Betsy-Tacy's Minnesota), offered an
organic lesson in the virtues of the simple life.

"Mommy, do you think that in certain ways, life was better
back then?" Beatrice asked one night.

"I often do," I replied, and she nestled in close on the sofa,
bound by a common sympathy. One night, as we read *Farmer
Boy*, Beatrice grew anxious as the three children in the story
played with forbidden sugar while their parents were away.

"Which character do you most identify with?" she asked me, all
atremble. "Eliza Jane," I answered. Eliza Jane was the sage one, the
one who tries to tamp down the wild rumpus and avert trouble.
"Me, too!" Beatrice agreed breathlessly. "What's going to happen
when their parents get home?" At times, Little House felt like an
especially effective parenting manual with its frequent homilies
on frugality, respect, resourcefulness, honesty, and gratitude.

Of course, there are limits to those lessons. My friend Alysia found the Little House books similarly instructive—for a time. "What do you think Laura would do in a situation like this?" she'd ask her nine-year-old daughter, as I occasionally did with Beatrice. This kind of moralizing was pleasingly successful until one day, at age ten, her daughter rolled her eyes and replied, "Mommy, those were olden times."

When Teddy was one and a half years old, and my other two were four and five, I got an e-mail from my friend Sam Tanenhaus, whom I'd met shortly after 9/11 at a luncheon for V. S. Naipaul and who was now the editor of the *New York Times Book Review*. Sam asked whether I knew anyone who'd like to be the children's books editor at the *New York Times*. The most recent editor had left after seven years and Sam was looking for suggestions to replace her. He knew about my penchant for Kidlit because I'd written an essay about it for the paper.

But I wasn't much use in the way he expected. My experience with children's literature had been as an enthusiast, not a professional. I didn't know many writers or editors in that world. None of my referrals worked out.

And then I had a kind of epiphany. While on a family vacation in Los Angeles, I was driving with my husband, our children in the backseat, trying to figure out how to get to Every Picture Tells a Story, an especially good children's bookstore and illustration gallery (sadly now gone), without having to bring the kids. They would only distract me from my mission. Michael and I were comparing our schedules when I realized what I was trying to do: go to a children's bookstore by myself. For myself. Without my children. That way I could look at the children's books *I* wanted to look at and not be distracted by their needs. Was this normal? If I cared so much about children's books, perhaps *I* should be the children's books editor.

The problem was I never wanted to work in an office again. The last time I'd worked in an office, I had a boss who docked my pay when I got invited to go on *Oprah* in Chicago to promote my first book. At the office I worked in before that, my boss required all employees to take a personality test that divided us neatly into one of four quadrants: Doers, Creators, Deciders, or Thinkers, categories that would then define our roles in the department. Most of the others were Doers; there were a couple of Deciders, too. I was the only Thinker. My first thought was, *I think I need to get out of here.*

When I'd left my last office job in 2002, I thought I'd left it for good. I'd finally managed to put together the professional life I'd always wanted. I was being paid to write. And I didn't have to wait to write in the evening after an exhausting workday, but could do it instead during regular business hours. The pragmatics of the freelance life were enormously appealing. You could spend the entire day in pajamas. You could fit in household chores between assignments. You could set your own hours. I figured as long as I could earn enough to offset the cost of childcare, I was in the black. Given how little writing pays, I worked like a maniac but I loved it.

Most of all, I loved being present at home with my children, fostering the kind of domestic sphere I'd longed for when I was a child. I could dip in and out to nurse them when they were babies and prepare their lunches when they moved on to solid food; cuddle them or peer in at the doorway, and then retreat to my home office, to report a story or bang away at whatever book I was working on. When they went to school, they never came home to an empty house. I knew this was a privileged lifestyle, and after years of wiping counters and folding Laura Ashley sweaters and apologizing on behalf of diners who lingered too long over their check and memorizing vegetable codes at the supermarket checkout, I appreciated it. Why would I ever leave a job like this?

But that day in LA, while plotting my visit to Every Picture Tells a Story, I sent an impulsive e-mail to Sam. "Maybe if the job could be part-time, I'd consider it myself," I wrote, accidentally Dick Cheneying my way into the position. Four weeks and several interviews later, to my surprise more than anyone else's, I was sitting at a desk overlooking West Fortieth Street. Though it took a while to realize it was not okay to wear maternity clothes to work when you were no longer pregnant, I'd found an office even better than the one I had at home. I was surrounded by other book-and-word people and they were all Thinkers. I felt like a kid given full run of the candy store. There were books everywhere, and they were mine. And I was working at the *New York Times*, a paper I'd read religiously ever since I was a child and my father had told me, "If you want to be an engaged citizen of the world, you have to read the *Times*."

Time with my children became, alas, yet more compressed. As for most parents who work outside the home, moments on either end of the workday grow precious. How to spend time together became a Math Olympiad–level calculation among competing options: homework, cello practice, conversation, dinner, family reading. Luckily, my kids took my employment in stride; they, too, wanted those books.

Not that they had ever suffered from literary want. From the beginning, I'd modeled my policy on book purchases after my father's, but with even less discipline. Essentially, I bought my kids all the books they wanted, plus books they didn't want but I did. Now they had yet more, including bound galleys of novels before they were published, which my kids soon recognized as priceless when it came to work by their favorite authors. I wasn't at home as often, but I was helping nurture a family of readers.

A year after she so coldly set aside *A Wrinkle in Time*, Beatrice picked it back up. This time, after rereading the first book, she continued straight through. When she put down the fifth and final volume, she turned to me with a mix of pity and disdain, disappointed in the children's books editor of the *New York Times*. "I can't believe you only read the first three books," she said. I also now understood why Beatrice hadn't needed *A Wrinkle in Time* as much as I did at her age. Since the 1970s, children's literature has expanded enormously for girls, and worthy female protagonists were everywhere. Beatrice met them all the time.

Every day, when I came home from work, carting my tote bags, my children greeted me by asking, "What books did you bring?" occasionally fighting over the latest installment of The Land of Stories or Rick Riordan. My older son, Tobias, a voracious and widely curious reader, was open to almost every story except sad ones; discovering new books for him was a source of constant joy. Teddy laughed over any funny books with an unrestrained glee; ferreting out these books became an ongoing and thoroughly rewarded quest. My family of readers told me which books worked and which ones didn't. They each contributed in their way to the *Book Review*, growing up knowing that their opinions mattered.

When, after two years, Sam left and I was asked to take his place as editor of the *Book Review*, abandoning my post as children's books editor, my kids looked stricken. There was no avoiding the facts: I'd been demoted.

CHAPTER 20

Bad News

Tearjerkers

Books make me cry all the time. I cry when I'm alone, I cry reading in the office. I cry when I read with my children, big sappy tears blotching up the pages. I cry in public, once snuffling loud and sloppily on the subway over Sonali Deraniyagala's wrenching and perfect memoir, *Wave*, in which her entire family succumbs to the 2004 tsunami, nearly unable to get off the train at my stop.

My Book of Books is full of such obvious weepies, but these aren't the only culprits. I also cry when a book makes me a little too happy. When it becomes dangerously heartwarming and tips into an unendurable joy, I start to lose it. It can even be a picture book: the end of Patrick McDonnell's *Me . . . Jane* where Jane Goodall wakes from her girlhood dream of one day working with animals and we turn the page to find the famous photograph of a baby chimpanzee reaching out to touch young Jane's hand. To want something so much, and then get it, to experience, even secondhand, that almost unimaginable reward. Without fail, I sob over Goodall's exquisite achievement, baffling my children. There goes Mommy crying over a book *again*, and it's not even sad!

I don't always wait for the ending. With Tomi Ungerer's *Otto: The Autobiography of a Teddy Bear* I started tearing up the moment I realized a stuffed animal was in peril. I'd profiled Ungerer for the *Times* in 2011, after which he signed three picture books for my children. For Teddy, he naturally chose *Otto*. Since Teddy was only two at the time, I stowed the book on a high shelf in his older brother's room. One night Tobias took it down. I hadn't preread the book, eager to first experience its pleasures in the company of my children. I was completely unprepared.

Otto: The Autobiography of a Teddy Bear is a story told, per its title, from the perspective of an aged stuffed animal, sitting in the window of an antiques shop. His ear is stained purple from juice spilled by his first owner, David, and we flash back to that little boy, growing up in Germany during World War II. When David, bearing a yellow star, is suddenly taken away (alarm bells!), he entrusts his beloved bear Otto to his best friend. In the tumult of war, Otto loses this owner as well. By now, I am dabbing my eyes, avoiding those of my children.

An American GI finds the abandoned Otto and holds him aloft as he is hit by gunfire; the bear's plush belly blocks the bullet, saving the soldier's life. Years pass and through this and that Otto winds up in an American antiques shop where David's best friend, now an old man, recognizes the stain. A newspaper hails the reunion. David, we discover, has survived the war, too, and reads the paper. We end with Otto bringing the two friends back together, by which point I am a blubbering mess.

According to Bob, the first book that made me completely lose it was Henry James's *The Portrait of a Lady*, which I read shortly after my divorce, taking every plot point personally, weeping over Isabel Archer's torments and tragedy. Rather than focus on the beauty of James's prose, I let myself get entirely caught up and then fall apart over the plot, continuing to cry even after I'd closed the book and put it away. But *Portrait of a Lady* is no exception. Novel after novel, things get soggy.

Perhaps this sentimentality could be fought off. "I will not cry over *The Fault in Our Stars*," I told myself before picking up John Green's tearjerker YA novel about two cancer patients, knowing exactly what I was in for. "It's too much of a cliché." Surely I could rise above the adolescent drama because I was approaching it from a professional angle as children's books editor. I would not be manipulated.

I cried like a brokenhearted fifteen-year-old.

In 2013, on the way back from visiting my cousin Kirsten, now living in London with her husband, I cried while reading *A Tree Grows in Brooklyn*. Alone on the plane to New York, my bathos took up several seats, covered with damp tissues. Two passengers and a flight attendant came over to ask if I was okay.

The following year, I took Beatrice and my mother along on my next trip to London. Beatrice was eight at the time, and had read enough about England to make a visit abroad meaningful, her very first bout of literary tourism. We had many lit-tour plans: the Harry Potter walking tour, the Harry Potter studio, the British Museum, the bookstores. Marchpane, a tiny store dedicated to used and rare children's books, many of them out of print. Daunt, a pair of stores that organize books according to geography, allowing browsers to tour a world of literature within its walls. Beatrice and I annoyed my mom by antisocially reading on the Tube exactly the way we read on the subway back home. We'd stake out seats as soon as we boarded and whip out our books, eschewing conversation.

One afternoon, after my mother ditched us for the Victoria and Albert Museum, Beatrice and I were on the Tube en route to meet friends at the Globe Theater. I was reading *Never Mind*, the first volume of the Patrick Melrose series, Edward St. Aubyn's autobiographical novels tracing his trajectory through boyhood, heroin addiction, and recovery. I'd wanted to read St. Aubyn's books after so many authors I admired had gushed about them in the *Book Review*'s "By the Book" column. "Have you read the Patrick Melrose books?" was the question everyone was asking that publishing season, and I was tired of saying, "Not yet."

Meanwhile, Beatrice was on an Enid Blyton tear. She'd read the few volumes of Blyton that had made their way stateside, English editions stickered over with American prices, but the supply had dried up. Blyton, who died in 1968, was wildly popular in Britain and throughout the Commonwealth for much of the twentieth century, but had taken a critical battering in later enlightened years on charges of sexism, racism, elitism, poor writing, and an absence of imagination. Some of the most egregious material has been sloughed off recent editions, which bear remarketed illustrations even as the content—boarding school shenanigans, old-fashioned capers, and fantasies—remains largely the same.

Our very first day in London, we went directly to my favorite bookstore in the city. If we hadn't, I'd just be counting the minutes until I did. Beatrice understood completely. Hatchards, founded in 1797, is the oldest bookshop in London, just off Piccadilly Circus. It's the official bookstore to the royal family; it actually feels like a bit of a privilege to shop there. A wooden staircase, buffed by age, winds up multiple floors, past displays featuring an idiosyncratic selection of literary fiction and stubbornly British subjects of concern. There is no café.

Beatrice, her undereyes mauve with fatigue, was nonetheless stirred awake by the store's bounty of Blyton. She pored over her options, plucking titles from the shelves into hopeful towers on the floor. The Hatchards salesperson kept giving us additional shopping bags and gold paper bookmarks as if we would somehow dematerialize if not adequately rewarded for our patronage. While there, I picked up the Patrick Melrose series, published here individually with muted pastel covers that telegraphed the melancholy contents within.

Beatrice had her books and I had mine. The first Patrick Melrose book, *Never Mind*, takes place over the course of a day in the life of a five-year-old boy from an aristocratic family: his mother, a drug-addled narcissist; his father, a sadist. The boy Patrick meanders about the family house in Provence, neglected by the adults who are supposed to care for him. When he is summoned by his father and sexually abused—a heartbreaker of a scene told entirely from the child's bewildered perspective—it's the most parental attention he ever gets.

Reading this on the train, I immediately choked up, and as our train pulled into our station I found it hard to make any sound, never mind the customary maternal chatter or parental exhortation. Beatrice was across from me, though far off in a very different corner of English literature with Blyton's St. Clare's series.

"Ack, our stop!" she cried in mild panic, looking up from her book as if at any moment the world outside could slip from her

MY LIFE WITH BOB

grasp. "I was at the best part!" She didn't have time to see my tears before they were wiped away. Certain stories children are not prepared to hear. Sometimes adults aren't either.

You would think that as we age, tales of other people's suffering wouldn't tug at us so insistently. In fact, the opposite can be true. The triggers are more numerous and more readily accessed, the losses felt more acutely. When you read about an injured child or an ignored brother or an estranged parent, you can more easily intuit their pain. Nostalgia goes from being a light feeling of déjà vu to something more primal and raw. The span of history constricts as decades-old horrors no longer seem quite so distant. When I was growing up, the Holocaust felt like ancient history; now it seems to have taken place yesterday.

The greater stakes can make every tragic plot turn ever more real and painful. In the second volume of the Melrose series, *Bad News*, Patrick is in his twenties and addicted to heroin. One very long night, while bingeing on an appalling mixture of substances, he receives a message from home that his estranged father, the man who tormented him throughout his childhood, has died. The bad news of the title is multifold: a father has died, a son has been nearly destroyed, their relationship has been poisonous from beginning to end, any possibility of reconciliation ruined.

On the surface, I had nothing in common with Patrick Melrose and his father had nothing in common with mine. But in that way of good fiction, *Bad News* prodded an uncomfortable personal question: What happens when an estranged parent dies? How do you tie up the complex emotions in a foreshortened amount of time? A deathbed reconciliation—too late, compromised, of questionable sincerity—might feel cheap or, worse, thwarted. There would be guilt, and regrets.

The year before, on New Year's Day, my father had been diagnosed with stage IV esophageal cancer. People aren't supposed to start dying when you're angry at them, and my dad and I had barely been on speaking terms for months. He certainly wasn't a monster like Patrick Melrose's father; on the contrary, for most of my life, he and I had been close. But over the previous year we'd had a near-total falling-out; at times I felt like I hated him and, worse, that he hated me. *Never do business with family* is such a sensible maxim, it's a wonder so few people follow it. I certainly didn't, and instead made the mistake of hiring my dad, a commercial contractor nearing retirement, to renovate my house in Harlem. How much time and money and headache I'd save, was the deluded thought going in.

Ten months of construction later, a period in which my family shuffled from floor to floor, fleeing dust and heavy demolition, cursing the construction workers who left behind a trail of half-empty Snapple bottles with cigarette butts swimming in the murk and child hazards everywhere—staircases without banisters, abrupt holes in the floor, rusty nails in the hallway—my father and I could barely tolerate each other.

Our tense exchanges occasionally flared into fights in which we'd forcefully denounce each other from across the living room. I feel horrendous about it now and felt dreadful then, even if everyone agreed he had become impossible.

I wish I could rewrite this part. My father had always been an irrepressible storyteller, refining and repeating cherished anecdotes over the years; I'd like to brush this story up. My father could have continued to be the same character he'd always been—the raconteur and the indulger and the practical joker. His final years could have been marked by a growing kinship, my father imparting wisdom to his grandchildren and sharing memories of his own childhood and parents. I'd be able to say that our mutual affection only deepened with time. This is the story I would have liked to write, and I would have been a better character in it, too, a solace and a sweetness to my father in his years of decline.

He had been deteriorating for a long time. About ten years earlier, there had been three botched knee surgeries, one of which involved a nasty case of drug-resistant staphylococcus. Once an avid tennis player and hiker, he was no longer able to walk farther than a block, perpetually in search of a bench. Everything slowed down, including his curiosity, no longer free to roam. His default position was to splay his increasingly overweight form into a recliner, from which he'd only emerge accompanied by a stream of loud exertions. When he wasn't complaining, he was coughing up a hair-raising amount of phlegm and spitting it out the car window to universal dismay.

In 2011 he had received a questionable diagnosis of Wegener's granulomatosis, a rare autoimmune disorder. Even though tests were never able to confirm the diagnosis, his doctors prescribed all manner of antibiotics and sedatives; he sometimes fell asleep while driving, once with my children in the backseat. No more picking the kids up from school. Unable to climb stairs but deep in denial, he stopped overseeing the construction work in my house. Problems mounted; so did costs.

A creeping black mold began to fester underneath the freshly installed, opalescent green tiles in my kids' newly renovated bathroom, creating dark garlands around their bottles of shampoo like an insidious omen. Each night, the murky growth wended its way beneath a new rectangle of artisanal, recycled glass, my one splurge in the renovation. "It's just the color of the glass!" my father repeated angrily every time I mentioned the sprawling decay. Or alternately, "It's settling in. That happens with tile over time!" The tile was three months old.

Sedated and autosuppressed, my father was no longer himself. Never what one would call an easy person, he had nonetheless been a character, the kind all my friends fell for and grew to love. People always wanted to spend Thanksgiving at our house, primarily, I think, for my father's company. Everyone who knew him felt tremendous affection, and relished his all too imitable mannerisms. My brothers and I called it "speaking in Jerry" and we did so regularly among ourselves. A lot of it was about the Brooklyn accent and the hand gestures, usually indicating fatigue or dismissal, but there were also a few key phrases, such as:

- **"I got Hank on the other line."** This was something you'd say when you needed to hang up the phone or were just ready to say good-bye. Hank was my father's construction supervisor and the two of them back-and-forthed all day, first on a walkie-talkie, then on a car phone, and finally by cell. For maximum effect, my brothers and I would say it the moment the other person had begun sharing something deep or meaningful.
- **"Horseshit!"** This we would cry out in response to anything perfectly acceptable and true. You would have to say it with a decisive note, end of discussion.
- **"Do you know what I find *fascinating*?"** This could be Ulster County cemeteries, time dilation, Rodgers & Hammerstein, Powell and Pressburger, Balinese handicrafts, or the crazy people who still attended meetings of the Lincoln Brigade. My brothers and I would use it as a preface to anything deserving of time and attention.

- **"Seriously, Pammy."** This is what my father did when he reprimanded me or delivered tough counsel. My brothers would use it to indicate I'd said something foolish.

As my father grew sicker with a disease he didn't know he had and increasingly medicated for a disease he probably didn't, his Jerryisms waned. He became depressed, less conversational, more easily frustrated, and prone to outbursts. When his own mother had been alive, he'd ridiculed her for her gratuitously explicit descriptions of physical ailments; now he offered up the same vivid detail. At first, we thought he was imitating her as a joke, but he either became serious over time or had been serious all along. I was regularly treated to a lurid blow-by-blow of his most recent colonoscopy or toenail gone awry.

In this last phase of life, he was routinely furious with someone who had wronged him. Increasingly, that person was me. After months of arguments, my father and I settled into a simmering détente. We would show up at the same family gatherings. We would communicate mostly through forcedly jovial exhortations to the children: "Look, it's Grandpa!!" (My kids adored him and needed little encouragement.) Then, over Christmas break in 2012, while on a family vacation in Vermont, my mother got a phone call from my stepmother in New York. My father was in the hospital. He could no longer swallow food. They were doing tests.

The ghastliness my father had been coughing up, it turned out, was cancer. But it wasn't diagnosed as such until it had spread from his esophagus to his liver, now so engorged with malignant tissue that it bulged out of his abdomen like a balloon. At the time of diagnosis, I hadn't seen my father for weeks. The last time we'd exchanged words was at his apartment during a holiday celebration for the grandchildren, when I noticed how much weight he'd lost. "I can't keep a thing down!" he said balefully, in what I assumed to be exaggeration for effect, before shuffling off to a lounge chair.

Upon returning from Vermont, I rushed to see him. Questions of wrongdoing and blame were moot; there was no time to negotiate the peace, it was simply assumed. He was no longer angry with me nor I with him. Our fight was over. We rode side by side to his next hospital visit in the backseat of my brother Brian's car, holding hands as we hadn't done since I was in elementary school. Chemo, the oncologist said, wouldn't cure my father and it probably wouldn't prolong his life either. Nonetheless, he recommended it. When I pressed the doctor for odds, he said the chemo had a 30 percent chance of working, though in the absence of curing or prolonging life I wasn't sure what working meant. "Tell me the truth," I said to the doctor in the hallway. "To me, it looks like he'll be dead in weeks." The doctor merely shrugged in response.

For two weeks, my father allowed visitors, and then he cut us all off. The last person to visit was Tobias, who spent an afternoon in his company. "I love that child so much," my dad told me in what I didn't know would be our last conversation. After that, he wouldn't even come to the phone, no matter how much my brothers and I pleaded. My stepmother and a hospice nurse cared for him in his apartment. Every day, I'd call my stepmother, begging to see him. It wasn't for my sake, it was for his. I had to tell him something. I had to tell him that I'd keep his stories alive forever, repeating them to his grandchildren so they would always know him. They would know that he played stickball in the streets of Brooklyn as a child and that his father, Tisme (nicknamed for answering the telephone with a spirited "Tis me!"), owned meat markets in the city. There really were meat-and-potatoes people; and these people were theirs.

I would tell them how Grandpa had wanted to go away to college, but had to stay home and commute to Hofstra, that he'd gone to law school but had to drop out when my mother got pregnant. I would tell them his stories about the corruption at Idlewild Airport ("You know, it wasn't always called JFK, Pammy!"), the wads of cash and the unions but also the excitement of taking part in the building of the city, and the pride he'd taken in the floor work he'd done for Delta Airlines.

My children would laugh as I always laughed when I told them about the practical jokes he'd played in the army, many of them centered on the latrine. They would love the story about how he and my stepbrother Nicky mixed up a batch of fake vomit and spilled it all over the apartment so that when my stepmother came home she panicked at the sight of her son wiped out on the floor in a mess. How he never tired of depositing rubber rats and cockroaches and snakes around the house in Woodstock, then lying in wait. How he could inexplicably and repeatedly watch the movie *Romy and Michele's High School Reunion*, never losing interest. "That Lisa Kudrow, she's really something," he'd tell me after each viewing, as if he'd only just discovered her himself.

I wanted to promise him I'd frame the photographs he and the kids took of each other when he let them order gigantic milk shakes at the City Diner, their faces coated in chocolate. I would remind them about his days carpooling them home from school and giving them white Tic Tacs and spare change. The way his own father, Tisme, would offer me Five-Flavor Life Savers when I saw him. Even if I could do nothing to alleviate my father's current pain, I needed him to know all of this, for him to hear it before he went. I had to convey the one message I could that would make him feel better.

"He doesn't want to see anyone," my stepmother said.

Finally, on the phone one night. I persuaded her to allow me to visit despite my father's objections. Check with her in the morning, she said. When I called Friday morning, she said, "He can't say no now." I rushed to their apartment, where my father lay on a hospital cot surrounded by the detritus of the ailing—the wet wipes and salves and tissues. Years of accumulated body mass had evaporated and what remained was sunken into the bedsheets. His eyes fluttered intermittently, their surfaces milky and gray. I held the bare sheath of his hand and squeezed it as I delivered my final message. He moaned occasionally while I spoke; there was no telling whether in response to my words or in response to something that existed only for him. The uncertainty broke my heart, but I kept talking, repeating the important part, over and over. "I love you, Daddy, and your grandchildren love you, too. I will make sure you remain alive for them and be their grandpa forever."

Then I went to work, where I dissolved into tears at the first friendly colleague I saw in the elevator. That night, at six o'clock, my stepmother called as I got out of the subway to say that my father was dead. It had been one month to the day between diagnosis and death.

After he died, my mind drifted. I would read pages over and over and over with eyes glazed. I wasn't actually reading. Bob remained on his shelf, untouched, for weeks. With effort, I finally turned to my usual memoirs, the sadder the better: Christopher Hitchens's *Mortality*, the writer's account of his diagnosis and last days of cancer. Jaycee Dugard's *A Stolen Life*, about her kidnapping and abuse. I needed to cry about someone else.

When I wasn't soaking in dark memoirs, I looked to my other standby for solace: classic English novels. There is something reassuring and necessary about home literature—the books you grow up with, the ones you were taught in school, the cultural touchstones you consider your own. For me, this has always meant the great books I'd looked up to from an early age. No matter where I am, no matter what's going on in my life, when I want something reliable, I reach for the Dickens, the Eliot, the Austen. The more boring the book title—*The Mill on the Floss, Silas Marner, Tess of the d'Urbervilles*—the more stalwartly I cling to the familiar contours of its contents.

These books have recognizable beginnings, middles, and ends. There's the primary couple and the secondary couple. The friends and the sidekicks and the comic relief, the measured ways in which coincidence, lost opportunity, and hard lessons are meted out. Even the plot twists are somehow predictable. Inside these pages, I feel tucked in and at ease knowing that such books exist and continue to exist, that their characters endure.

In an unfortunate twist worthy of Hardy or Wharton, my father died a month before I became the editor of the *Book Review*. He'd taken such pride in my working for the *Times*. He took every chance to boast about it to friends, as if he'd had a hand in my success. Well, he had.

How happy he would have been to see me finally have all the books I wanted. To know that his indulgence at the Roosevelt Field Barnes & Noble had paid off. That he'd helped start something and nurture it along the way. When I look through the galleys as they arrive at the *Book Review*, I still feel the impulse to grab every new book about the Spanish Civil War or Catskills history, the latest John le Carré, the books he loved. When I read these books, I read them for him.

CHAPTER 21

Les Misérables

Why Read?

Not so long ago at a Kidlit book club gathering, one of our members asked a question that stopped us all: "Why do you read?" She asked this during an animated debate about the relative merits of the book under discussion (a children's book, of course), one that had inspired widely divergent reactions. It may be that we responded to the book so differently, she implied, because we were after different things.

"I'm serious," she repeated. She happens to be a psychologist, so naturally she pressed us to really think about our answers. "Why do you read?'

This was asked of a group of hard-core book people. Most of us were literary agents, English teachers, editors, or authors. We should have known the answer more or less by heart. Yet each of us looked slightly dumbstruck, as if we'd been forced to gaze inward and justify our very existence on the spot. It was obvious. Why hadn't anyone thought to ask this question before? We paused to think. Then we went around the table and took turns giving answers.

"I read for sheer entertainment."

"I read to learn."

"I read to make sense of the world."

"I read to find out something new."

"I read to escape."

"I read because it makes me happy."

"I read for discovery."

For each of us, there seemed to be one core need that drove us to read on. But it was more complicated than that, as the ensuing conversation soon revealed. Everyone experiences most of these urges at different moments, or during certain periods of our lives, which is why most good readers read widely, even if they tend to go deep into one genre or another.

And one's primary reason for reading can shift over time, sometimes quite suddenly. A death, a divorce, an empty nest, a health crisis—these kinds of life changes might pivot that central motivation. Not surprisingly, several people at the dinner table offered tiered answers. "I used to read because I was looking for answers, but now that I've reached middle age, I fundamentally read for pure enjoyment," one person explained. "I'm no longer looking for confirmation," another said. "I want to be challenged."

When it was my turn, my first answer was, "I read to be transported." It has always been this way. At base, I want to enter a world apart. To take off. Perhaps it's that insecure desire left over from childhood—the wondering what it would be like to be someone else, some other kind of heroine, pursuing adventures more worthy and interesting than my own. Given the chance, I want to go elsewhere in time, place, perspective—whether to present-day Algeria or 1980s Montana or pre-Code Hollywood.

It's not exactly about escape. It's about experiencing something I would otherwise never have the chance to experience. To know what it's like to be a merchant marine in the South Pacific precisely because I never will be a merchant marine in the South Pacific. To experience a Norwegian boyhood in the early twentieth century like Roald Dahl's because I would otherwise never know what it meant to grow up just outside the Arctic Circle, to walk miles to get to the nearest dentist, to be beaten with a cane by a cruel headmaster. Books answer that persistent question, "What is that really *like*?" By putting you in the place of a character unlike yourself in a situation unlike your own, a good book forges a connection with the other. You get to know, in some way, someone you never would have otherwise known, to live some other life you yourself will never live.

This is probably why I rarely feel the urge to turn to fiction about contemporary American family dysfunction or the saga of someone working for a newspaper in New York or doing the old work-life-family tango. Maybe because I live it, I don't exactly find it gripping material. Or especially enlightening. The *Norton*-driven need to fill in the gaps and accumulate knowledge, however fleeting, still percolates within, insatiable. I'd rather know more about what I don't already know.

In November 2015, I returned to Paris for the first time in eight years. With the advent of e-mail and Skype, staying in touch with the Mathieus electronically would have been easy, but we almost never corresponded. Though it's difficult to achieve with a full-time job and three children, I far preferred to maintain the relationship through physical presence and place. It was a relationship founded in total immersion and identification, and keeping it that way felt right. I hadn't been to Paris since I was pregnant with Teddy, a trip marred by horrendous morning sickness. On one especially surly afternoon, I'd stomped around the city in search of something decent to eat; the only thing I could tolerate was bitter dark chocolate ice cream *without hazelnut*. Why was there nothing to eat in Paris?

My French sister, Juliette, now a biogeneticist at the Institut Pasteur, had come to visit during a conference in New York a few years earlier; since then, she'd had two children. The apartment where I'd stayed as a student was now hers. My French brother, Paul, had become an architect like his father, married his Romanian girlfriend, and had three kids. He'd been fourteen when I lived there; now his hair was gray, and he lived within walking distance of the atelier he shared with Bertrand. The youngest Mathieu, Margot, only ten when I first lived in Paris—the same age as Beatrice—had moved to Brussels with her husband and two children, where she worked as a child psychologist. There were seven brand-new Mathieus and I'd never met any of them.

From the airport I went directly to their house forty minutes north of Paris. By happy circumstance, Margot was visiting from Belgium. There was a street fair in town that weekend, a crowded warren of wares that bore an unsettling resemblance to the street fairs on Third Avenue in Manhattan—the same standardized junk food and Chinese imports, punctuated only occasionally by dollops of French culture—crepes, "follies" of bonbons, artisanal cheese.

In some ways, the place hadn't changed. The Mathieus' house was still a ramshackle jumble, walls covered in giant antique mirrors, corners cluttered with the same faded vacation photographs of La Rochelle, immense wooden bookshelves teeming with Éditions Gallimard, an entire ceiling in the parlor dangling with Carole's fantastical chandeliers—baroque antiques she'd embellished with Belgian glass crystals she'd bought *"pas trop cher"* from a friend. It was the kind of house where you constantly bumped into a memory. A nineteenth-century pepper grinder. Ancient copies of *Le Monde*. A grandparent's handmade doll.

"I'm reading this Icelandic author," Carole enthused, foisting a French translation in my direction. "You must see if they're translated into English." (They were not.) A diplomat from the Ivory Coast, in town for a Euro-African cultural congress, came by for lunch the same day I arrived. They'd all known one another as students. Bertrand had held on to a copy of his friend's doctoral thesis. The diplomat pleaded for it back, but Bertrand genially refused. "You gave this to me as a gift! It's a work of genius and it's precious to me—you cannot have it." Everyone drank aperitifs in the garden while Margot's toddlers played in the grass, lightly ignored the way small French children often are.

But the Mathieus' world had changed in other ways. On Sundays, when most pharmacies are closed, the owners post signs to direct people in case of emergency to the one pharmacy open. Having remembered to buy a few toiletries I'd naturally forgotten to pack, I found myself that Sunday in a pharmacy in an unfamiliar part of town. Here amid the indistinct high-rises of low-income housing, the women wore headscarves; groups of men gathered on corners and street crime was common. I'd been shocked earlier that year when, after the *Charlie Hebdo* massacre, the fugitives allegedly took refuge in this medieval walled city surrounded by farmland, forest, and an old sugar factory, of all places. The village's residents were not surprised.

Carole had cleared out three rooms on the third floor for a family of Syrian refugees, a young couple with a one-year-old. She'd installed a makeshift kitchen and left a pile of hand-me-downs from her seven grandchildren. "As long as they aren't Muslim," the woman before her in line told the village committee looking for families willing to accept placements. "We only want to take in Christian refugees."

"We'll take anyone, *even* if they're Christians," Carole informed the committee when it was her turn, a story she repeated with mischievous glee.

I spent the rest of the week in the old apartment on rue Rambuteau, leaving reluctantly Thursday night. The following day at work, the shocking headlines tore across my computer screen. Dozens of people had been killed at the Bataclan concert hall not far from the Marais. It was Friday, November 13, and Paris had again exploded in terrorist violence. Facebook quickly confirmed that all the Mathieus were okay. But what had happened to their city? What had happened to the city that I couldn't help but think of as partly my own?

The book I turned to was Victor Hugo's 1862 masterpiece, *Les Misérables*. I hadn't read a single French novel for two decades, not since taking a French lit course at the Alliance Française in my twenties, before my brain got tired. When the class was over, I fully intended to come back to French novels— but only in French. *Why read in translation when I can read them in the original?* I reasoned. The result was I didn't read them at all. But after Juliette told me she'd finished Zola's entire oeuvre while pregnant, I decided I'd waited long enough. If I waited to read Zola and Hugo and Balzac in French, I'd be waiting another two decades.

That's how long I'd been meaning to read *Les Misérables*, a book I first encountered, as many people do, in musical form. When I arrived in Paris as a college student in 1992, my closest college friend, Victoria, and our other roommates and I decided to see the French version, then playing at the Théâtre Mogador. I had never read the book nor seen the show in English. I understood about a third of what was happening onstage, which naturally didn't stop me from bawling throughout. I immediately purchased the cast album in French and, when I got back to campus, stuck the cassette in my car and left it there for the entire year, driving everyone who had the misfortune to ride in my car insane with rage. "Don't you have anything other than that stupid French musical tape in your car?" they'd plead. Further marring the passenger experience, tears would inevitably stream down my cheeks as I drove along, quietly singing in French to myself. It took about three bars of an orchestral swell to get me going; I might still be in the driveway.

So fine, I was a bit of a *Les Miz* fan. I next saw the musical in Czech with my cousin Kirsten in Prague, and after much snobbish resistance—how could it possibly work in English?—I decided to see it on Broadway. "Only if you promise me not to mention a single time how much better it is in French," Michael warned me before consenting to come along. We watched the movie version together, too, both of us weeping unabashedly at the moment of Jean Valjean's redemption. When I deemed Beatrice old enough, I watched it with her. Then we watched it again. All three of my children groan when I get choked up just describing one of the songs.

Yet I resisted the novel. It wasn't just its formidable length. Or that the thought of reading it in French made me want to lie down. It was that I already knew what happened. Could I get through thirteen hundred pages when I could anticipate every impending catastrophe? Jean Valjean's onerous imprisonment for stealing a loaf of bread. The devastating abandonment of Fantine. The decision to entrust Cosette to the treacherous Thénardiers. Every plot point or at least the musical rendition of those plot points was something I'd idiotically sung to myself dozens of times. Was it possible to enjoy a novel when you knew the whole story in advance?

There was only one way to find out. The book, unlike the musical, begins with the bishop Myriel in a portrait of moral goodness so powerful it had me in tears within pages. In the musical, Bishop Myriel is the man who offers refuge to the paroled Jean Valjean when no one else will shelter him, then covers up his crime when Valjean steals the bishop's silver. It is the bishop who sets Valjean on the path to redemption when he tells him that he must consecrate his life to God. In the musical, Myriel has a single scene. In the book, he has an entire life. I read on.

Nothing could diminish the novel's drive. Though I knew nearly everything that would happen, I didn't know how it would play out. Each fateful decision filled me with trepidation and urgency. "No, Fantine!" I wanted to cry out as I read. "Stay away from that seductive young man!" As Alfred Hitchcock once said of suspense: You can have two men sitting at a table when a bomb suddenly goes off, momentarily frightening the audience. Or, far more effective, you can have two men sitting at the table and show the audience there's a bomb ticking under the table. The men continue to talk about baseball. The audience, complicit, is aware of what's going to happen. "Don't talk about baseball!" you want to shout. "There's a bomb under the table!"

Knowing everything ahead in *Les Misérables* only prolonged the anticipation and heightened the emotion. The attenuated suspense was at times almost unbearable, like helplessly watching trains collide in slow motion.

For me, in that moment in time, this book had everything. There was refuge to be found in Myriel's goodness, solace in Jean Valjean's earned redemption, comfort in Cosette's happy ending. I was transported to another world in a way that enriched the quality of my own. At the end of each day (it was too heavy to lug on the train), I could remove myself from the details of quotidian existence—the health care forms, the Valentine's Day cupcakes, the work meeting—for altogether different challenges: How to ensure a child's well-being when you cannot provide for her. How to forgive a father you never knew and how to forgive a father you knew well. How to pursue love without hurting other loved ones in the process. There was even a chapter featuring my thoroughly recognizable rue Rambuteau.

In place of childcare arrangements and deadline decisions, I could occupy my mind with larger questions: Can man change the course of his own life and the lives of others? How can religion both repress and uplift? How do revolutions succeed?

There were startling parallels between the post-Revolution tumult of France of nearly two hundred years earlier and the political and religious divides seizing Paris and the world today.

In an extended aside about the dangers of monasteries, Hugo decried the effects of religious fanaticism. Hugo was "for religion and against religions," referring to monastic life as "the scourge of Europe." He denounced "the violence so often done to the conscience, coerced vocations, feudalism relying on the cloister . . . the sealed lips, the immured minds, so many ill-fated intellects confined in a dungeon of eternal vows, the taking of the habit, souls buried alive." Centuries collapsed in his words.

The proper response, Hugo wrote, was to resist the tide of superstition and fight back against fanaticism and militarism. He was writing about Paris then, and he was also writing about Paris now, even elucidating aspects of the political and socioeconomic divides that trouble America today. Everything in this book resonated for me.

Victor Hugo, the great romantic historian of a novelist, French counterpart to Charles Dickens, understood the effects of inevitable change on a place you know and love, even as your memory clings to the familiar contours of its past. Writing about himself in the third person, he explains:

> Since he left it, Paris has been transformed. A new city has grown up that is, as it were, unknown to him. Needless to say, he loves Paris. Paris is his spiritual home. . . . All those places you do not see any more, that you may never see again and that you have kept a picture of in your mind, take on a melancholy charm; they come back to you with the mournfulness of an apparition, make the holy land visible to you, and are, so to speak, the very embodiment of France. And you

love them and you conjure them up as they are, as
they were, and you persist in this.

You can call up maps of Victor Hugo's Paris online and compare them to those of the city today; the outlines are all still visible, many of the streets are the same. You can trace Jean Valjean's
path across the city in 1832 and follow the same route today with
few detours. His Paris is still recognizable. I promised myself I
wouldn't let another eight years go by without returning to my
Mathieus and to my Paris. If reading *Les Misérables* couldn't
make me feel like the world was a safer place, it could at least
ground the current moment in a continuum.

The Internet also led me directly to Jean Valjean, or rather to
the American actor playing him in the London production. When
my family and I traveled to London the following year, that actor
invited Beatrice and me backstage after a performance. He had listened to me discuss *Les Misérables* on my *Times* books podcast
and reached out via Twitter. The three of us toured the dressing
rooms and costume area and walked the stage of the Queen's Theatre, Beatrice wearing Javert's immense black police hat. She was
ecstatic and overwhelmed seeing a character from a story come
alive and walking in his footsteps. I knew exactly how she felt.

CHAPTER 22

A Spy Among Friends

Other Writers

Encounters with various characters and authors now occur with some regularity, but they are no less affecting. When someone magically crosses the divide between page and life it still summons a sense of awe, like the Tooth Fairy suddenly made real.

And it happens when I least expect it. On one of our regular family trips to Los Angeles, where my husband grew up, I brought Ben Macintyre's true-life espionage tale, *A Spy Among Friends*, so I could give it to my in-laws when I was done. I'd inherited an obsession with spies from my father—John le Carré and Alan Furst and various historical accounts weave their way in and out of Bob's pages, continuing to connect the two of us through stories. Now that my father was gone, I felt lucky to share this interest with my in-laws, also Macintyre fans.

On a recent flight to LA, I came across a curious passage. Macintyre was describing the social scene in Beirut where Kim Philby, one of the infamous Cambridge Five ring of spies, was posted for a time. Philby was closest there with two other spy families, the British Elliotts and the American Copelands, neither of whom suspected he was a double agent working for Moscow.

The story was one of absolute betrayal—against country, against social class and family, against friends. For years, Philby had lied to his childhood companions and sworn colleagues, people whose families stretched back generations together, and conspired with the Soviets against them, putting all of their lives at risk. In an aside, Macintyre noted that Philby's Beirut neighbor, the longtime CIA agent Miles Copeland, also happened to be the father of Stewart Copeland, the former drummer of the Police. At night in Beirut, while the adults drank copiously and spied against one another, their children played together innocently underfoot. Young Stewart had apparently become good friends with Kim Philby's kids.

Having come of age in the eighties, I had all kinds of adolescent feelings about the Police. I remembered one afternoon in fifth grade when my friend Ericka, who was always more pop-culturally advanced, expertly inserted the Police into her portable cassette player while we suntanned in her backyard; it was the first pop music I'd ever listened to as an activity in and of itself. Later, we studied the band's full MTV repertoire, discovered *Lolita* through their lyrics, and religiously attended Sting concerts.

I hadn't listened to the Police in decades. But over dinner in Los Angeles, when I told my in-laws about *A Spy Among Friends*,

I mentioned the Copeland connection for the benefit of the other Gen Xers at the table.

"You probably don't know who Stewart Copeland is," I apologized to my father-in-law, who had decidedly not spent the eighties listening to the Police while suntanning.

"I know exactly who Stewart Copeland is," he replied. "He lives around the corner."

Two days later, I was hanging out in Stewart Copeland's studio while he showed me photographs of his parents' house in Beirut and told stories about the Philby kids. He had a copy of one of his father's books, blurbed by Philby himself from exile in Moscow. Everything in the book felt more immediate.

Such experiences are a sharp departure from the cloistered-reading life I'd experienced as a child. Now the subjects and authors regularly make their way into real life. No more need to stalk the Spalding Grays; my Book of Books is peopled with authors I have met on one occasion or another. In this new, still surreal reading life, I have found myself chatting at a dinner party with Christopher Hitchens, the man who once helped me take down Paul Johnson. I have e-mailed with Salman Rushdie, the man who once opened me up to global literature.

Each of these encounters still feels like an occasion. Meeting famous people can be awkward, especially people who are famous in the way that feels meaningful to me, which is to say writers. My inner fangirl is alive and well, making run-ins with the novelists I grew up on especially overwhelming. One weekend a few years ago, I bumped into Judy Blume, north star of the children's library, in the bathroom at the Miami Book Fair, where I was moderating a panel of authors.

"Why didn't you get her autograph?" Beatrice practically shouted when I told her about it a few months later, after she'd entered her own Blume phase.

"She was coming out of the toilet stall," I said.

Truthfully, seeing this apparition from my childhood inner world also had an almost stupefying effect. What could I say to her that hadn't already been said? It was hard not to be struck into dumb silence. The day after I told Beatrice this story, she and I were running errands on the Upper West Side when whom should we see but Judy Blume rushing up the sidewalk; Beatrice also went nearly speechless with shock. This time, not wanting to let her down, I stopped to say hello. But Blume had just gotten a manicure and so Beatrice couldn't get an autograph then either. For both of us, Judy Blume retained her status as a star at somewhat of a remove.

I'd met other authors before I started working at the *New York Times Book Review*, but this was under markedly different circumstances. As a freelance writer, most of the other writers I'd known personally were far below the ranks of Hitchens and Rushdie and Blume. We were more observers than participants and most of us were still just starting out. Like all authors, we desperately wanted our books to be reviewed (but only kindly, please), and were cowed by those charged with such decisions. None of us had won awards or written bestsellers at the time; most of us worked in isolated pockets of the five boroughs, typing away at manuscripts around the edges of day jobs and other assignments.

This kind of lonely work wasn't always easy and it certainly didn't feel glamorous. Writers often prefer to write alone but adore complaining together. And so a group of us banded together and met once a month to do just that. There was no need for us to do any reading or writing for our meetings; what we needed was commiseration.

We called ourselves the Invisible Institute. That's how we felt, and to a certain degree that's how we wished we could be if it weren't for the fact that we simultaneously wanted people to read our work. Each of us had at least one book or contract under our belt; even so, we were far from sanguine about the process. One woman had seen her book of war reportage cranked out by a major publisher and left to wither on the back shelves with nary a bookstore reading or review. Another saw her book "orphaned," the term used to describe what happens when an editor moves to another publishing house, leaving books in progress in the hands of a different editor, one who may hate the subject matter, dislike the author personally, or simply have no time to work on it. The Invisible Institute author in question was orphaned again, and again.

Here was a place to share those tales of woe. If a member's article or book was overlooked or insulted, we were all on his or her team against the forces of darkness—editors who didn't e-mail back when you proposed a story idea, assignments that went to other people, proposals that were rejected. There are all kinds of things to feel bad about when you're a writer, from poorly attended book parties to no book parties, from books hidden in the back of the store to books not even stocked in the store, from bad book reviews to no book reviews, and writers are notoriously sensitive creatures. But we Invisibles knew we were also lucky. Many writers toil away unpublished for years and our work was at least getting out there. Even so, most of us were working double and triple jobs, pumping out stories about eye cream to pay for stories about health care or teaching three classes on the side or producing radio pieces for scant wages. Writing doesn't pay, with the average fee per word lower today than it was in 1970—without being adjusted for inflation. We leaned on one another heavily in what felt like a precarious situation.

What could be more consoling than to know you weren't the only writer out there plagued with doubt, envy, hard-to-articulate yearnings, and plain old nerves? I was never going to leave the Invisible Institute, ever. But once I became editor of the *Book Review*, I had to. I'd joined the other side and could not in good conscience or without conflict of interest continue on their team. The Invisibles threw me one last dinner party and then went on without me; no doubt I am now held accountable for any negative or nonexistent reviews among their members.

Basically, this made me a traitor. At least, I feel like one. As the editor of the *New York Times Book Review*, I now know whether my friends' books are being reviewed before they do, and whether the review will make them cry. Having cried over reviews myself, I also know exactly how that feels. Yet here, on the other side, my priorities have to be different, no matter how much I appreciate an author as a reader or as a human being. I can't help when a less than favorable review comes in, nor can I ensure that the editors handling books written by my friends will find them worthy of assignment. At the *Book Review*, we can cover only about 1 percent of those books published in a given year. It's often a very tough call. Like all book-review editors, I necessarily have to view books as something to be sifted through and sorted, wheat separated from chaff, galleys tossed into dumpsters, unreviewed books sold to booksellers.

The process echoes those painful inventory nights, tossing

stripped books into the garbage at B. Dalton, only now I'm the one ordering the books dumped. And so it goes. The *Book Review* is meant to serve readers, to point them to the most important and best-written books of the season, and to preserve the opinions of our critics. While worthy books are overlooked all the time, I have to keep my sympathies and sorrys to myself.

That's not my only betrayal. Sometimes it is now I who "strip" books out of my life. I finally own so many that on occasion I turn to my collection and, as if on Tinder, scan my eyes over the shelves, swiping left on books that I then peel away from their companions and set aside for donation—to a library, a school, a friend. Getting rid of books, harshly brushing them away in favor of other titles, something I never thought I'd do. Where is my loyalty? My devotion to the book, to *all* books?

It's jarring to remember a time, not so long ago, when all I wanted was to own those books, to be among the writers who wrote them, to be a part of this world, a hope so inarticulable, so fundamental, so all-important that I could barely admit it to myself, let alone to other people. For a long time, I tried to content myself with reading other writers; I didn't quite realize I'd become one.

Now that I'm a writer as much as a reader, I realize the two aren't so different after all. This isn't to say that there aren't exceptional writers or that being a writer isn't an achievement, but rather that the achievement is more common than I'd once supposed. Aren't we all writers these days? We live through text. With our status updates and our e-mails, many of us spend our days writing down more words than we speak aloud. Anyone can write a book or post a story and find readers. Even those whose book reviews live exclusively on Amazon or Goodreads or in diaries or in the text of e-mails are still active creators of the written word.

All of us are writers reading other people's writing, turning pages or clicking to the next screen with pleasure and admiration. All of us absorb other people's words, feeling like we have gotten to know the authors personally in our own ways, even if just a tiny bit. True, we may also harbor jealousy or resentment, disbelief or disappointment. We may wish we had written those words ourselves or berate ourselves for knowing we never could or sigh with relief that we didn't, but thank goodness someone else has.

Ultimately, the line between writer and reader blurs. Where, after all, does the story one person puts on a page end and the person who reads those pages and makes them her own begin? To whom do books belong? The books we read and the books we write are both ours and not ours. They're also theirs.

This makes all of us spies among friends. When we read, we are spying on someone else's imagination and inhabiting it; the authors and their characters are momentarily our friends, even if they betray us, or we them. Even if we dislike the book or give it a negative review or give the book away when we're done. We peer into the lives they lived and the lives they conjured out of observation and inventiveness, dipping into them and then departing from their pages, taking with us what we will.

Epilogue

The Lives We Read

Because what people read says so much about them, I can't help wanting to know what other people are reading. Most of us do this. We crane our necks into our neighbor's personal space on the subway and pretend to tie our shoes so we can see the title that person is holding while standing in line. We try to decipher what's happening on someone else's tablet and iPhone. E-readers are especially noxious in their opacity. You want to blurt out, "Can you please just show me the cover? I need to know."

This results in a lot of what-are-you-looking-at looks. Mind your own business. But in my case, at least, this *is* my business and I can't. The moment someone lets me into his or her home, my gaze veers to the bookshelves, forming impressions of people I don't know and discovering unknown aspects of people

I thought I knew well. Is the person an alphabetizer? Does she have a thing for historical novels? Do the books appear suspiciously on display for show—distinguished spines and ornamental jackets, artfully selected for the color of the binding, nary a bad movie guide in their midst?

It's hard not to wish that everyone—my friends, my family members, writers I know and don't know—would keep a Book of Books. What better way to get to know them? You could find out so much if you could get a read on where other people's curiosities lie and where their knowledge is found: What are you reading? And what have you read? And what do you want to read next? Not knowing the answers to these questions means you miss a vital part of a person, the real story, the other stories—not the ones in their books, but the stories that lie *between* book and reader, the connections that bind the two together.

And the stories that bind readers to one another. Reading may be solitary, but in the aggregate books unite us. Stories allow us to share other people's experiences communally—across schools and cities, countries and languages. When a child in Uganda reads the same life-changing novel that the thirtysomething lawyer recalls reading while growing up in Illinois, a connection is established across class, culture, and time.

I'd like to think others would get as much out of a Book of Books as I have gotten out of mine. For each of us, the books we've chosen across a lifetime reveal not only our evolving interests and tastes, but also our momentary and insatiable desires, the questions we can't stop asking, the failings we recognize in ourselves at the time, and the ones we can see clearly only years later. We pass our lives according to our books—relishing and reacting against them, reliving their stories when we recall where

MY LIFE WITH BOB

we were when we read them and the reasons we did. Most people, I'm convinced, are not just searching for cocktail-party fodder when they ask what someone else is reading. They are trying to figure someone out, to get to the bottom of him. They are looking for clues.

My clues are all here, on these pages. On the pages of my Book of Books. When I look through Bob, the actual stories between his mottled covers may have been written by others, but they belong to me now. Nobody else on the planet has read this particular series of books in this exact order and been affected in precisely this way. Each of us could say the same about our respective reading trajectories. Even if we don't keep a physical Book of Books, we all hold our books somewhere inside us and live by them. They become our stories.

Acknowledgments

With my previous books, I had many people to thank who helped me with research and interviews. This book is different in that I only had to look inward and "interview" myself. I still needed lots of help. I want to thank everyone involved in the editing and publishing process: Paul Golob and Gillian Blake, Tracy Locke and Patricia Eisemann, Maggie Richards and Stephen Rubin. This is my fourth book with Henry Holt and they make clear why editors and publishing houses matter. I couldn't be more grateful for the passion, intelligence, and dedication they bring to the hard work they do. Thank you to my agent, Lydia Wills, the best, who found me this editorial home.

At the *New York Times*, I am lucky to have a boss who loves to read and loves books. My gratitude to Dean Baquet, who always asks, "What are you reading?" and almost always has a better answer than I do. I want to thank all my colleagues at the *Times*, especially at the *Book Review*. I get to spend my days with the smartest book people I know. I feel like I have the best job in the world, and I have Sam Tanenhaus to thank for that opportunity.

Some poor souls read this book in embryonic form and I thank them for their forbearance: the extremely talented Trish Hall, my dear old friend Mindy Lewis, my mother-in-law, Debra Stern, my still best friend, Ericka Tullis, my brilliant editor friend Vanessa Mobley. I must take a moment to say that my colleagues and friends Susan Dominus and Sarah Lyall are geniuses and I feel fortunate to know them and to have persuaded them to read this book. You couldn't ask for more precise or insightful editorial suggestions. They know how not to make you feel bad about bad writing. They also are surely responsible for any stylistic flair on these pages. Please read everything they write.

I want to thank my family, especially my late father and my brother Roger, the big galoot. Here is what I say to you: E.

Michael, Beatrice, Tobias, and Theodore: The only thing I didn't enjoy about writing this book was the time it took away from you. I hope it gives something back to you someday, because you are my everything.